To Dr. Arnolt
with best wishes
F. Bahrampour
April 22, 1971

IRAN:

THE EMERGENCE OF A MIDDLE EASTERN POWER

THE CORONATION

IRAN:

Emergence of a Middle Eastern Power

by FIROUZ BAHRAMPOUR

Director of International Relations Section
University of Tehran

THEO. GAUS' SONS, INC.
Brooklyn, N. Y. 11201

TO THE MEMORY

OF

MY FATHER

TABLE OF CONTENTS

Foreword 9

Preface 11

Introduction 15

I. HISTORICAL HERITAGE 17

II. CULTURAL CHARACTERISTICS 23

III. ACHIEVEMENTS OF REZA SHAH 29

IV. ACHIEVEMENTS OF MOHAMMAD REZA SHAH 32

V. GOVERNMENT AND POLITICS 37

VI. SOCIAL LIFE AND ORGANIZATION 48

VII. PROBLEMS OF ECONOMIC DEVELOPMENT 56

VIII. IRAN IN WORLD AFFAIRS 63

IX. CONCLUSIONS 71

Selected Bibliography 77

Appendices 79

Index 123

Foreword

IRANIAN HISTORIANS trace the origins of Iranian culture and civilization to the ancient Achaemenid and Sassanid periods of history. They are proud of the achievements of the Safavids, and in Iranian history, the Safavid era is known as the Golden Age. Iranians today find inspiration in the achievements of the past and this gives them confidence about the future of their country.

While the ancient and medieval history of Iran is resplendent with great accomplishments, as in the case of other Muslim Empires, a period of stagnation and decline started after the 17th century which lasted until recent times.

The 19th century was a period in which Iran found itself under pressure from the Russians in the north and the British in India to the south. The Qajar rulers were not able to cope with the domestic and foreign problems that beset them, and conditions deteriorated until the partially successful 1906 constitutional movement gave hope for a better future. Unfortunately, Iran found itself divided into spheres of influence by the 1907 Anglo-Russian Convention. While attempting to remain neutral in the First World War, the country was overrun by the belligerent powers. The period of instability and chaos following the end of the war, and the inability of Ahmad Shah Qajar and his Ministers to meet the crisis, resulted in the rise of Reza Shah Pahlavi, who was able to gain power, and from 1925 to 1941 introduced effective reforms and brought order and prosperity to Iran.

The present study deals primarily with recent Iranian history and the emergence of Iran as a modern state under the leadership of Mohammad Reza Shah Pahlavi. In the cycle of history, the present era is considered the beginning of a new period of accomplishment and progress. It is expected that the 1970's will be decisive in the destiny of the Iranian people. If one may judge from past Iranian history, we may now expect another period of flowering of culture and civilization in that country.

HARRY N. HOWARD*

* Dr. Harry N. Howard teaches Middle Eastern Affairs at the American University School of International Service in Washington, D.C. and is associated with the Middle East Institute. He is a retired Foreign Service Officer and is an authority on Middle Eastern history.

Preface

THE MAIN PURPOSE of this book is to help strengthen the already cordial relations existing between Iran and the United States. It is the author's hope that an analytical survey of Iran's relations with the United States since the dawn of this century, will be helpful to policy makers of both countries, and will be of interest to students of international affairs. While the emphasis is on the areas of mutual interest and cooperation, disagreements which in the past led to friction are also mentioned.

This study is not intended to be a detailed work dealing with the history, politics, and social structure of Iran. This essay is rather an attempt at an interpretation of modern Iranian history, analyzing recent developments in order to clarify Iranian policies and explain the reason for recent trends in Iran's internal and external affairs. For those interested in a comprehensive and detailed coverage of particular aspects of Iranian life, the footnotes and selected bibliography include the more useful sources.

The Middle East was an area of conflict and instability during the 19th and early 20th centuries as it is today. The emergence of a united and effectively administered Middle Eastern nation such as Iran in this important region of the world will no doubt serve the cause of peace. A strong Iran will be able to improve relations with all its neighbors, as well as with other nations, both large and small. While Iran's policy is one of peace at home and peace abroad, it

11

must be stressed that in times of crisis, the Iranian leadership has effectively met external threats, even against overwhelming odds, as was the case during the 1945-46 Azerbaijan confrontation. Iranians have not forgotten that during this critical time the United States and the United Nations came to the aid of their country. It is thus, natural for Iran to be a staunch friend of the United States and an active member of CENTO. On the other hand, astute Iranian diplomacy has in recent years improved relations with the USSR, in line with Iranian policy of living in peace with all nations.

At this writing, the possibility of British withdrawal in 1971 from the strategically and economically important Persian Gulf area is creating concern in the Free World about the security of this vital region. The United States, tied down in a long-drawn out struggle in Vietnam and the Far East, and also facing problems in many other parts of the world, is naturally not anxious to become involved in the Persian Gulf region. I contend that to the extent that Iran can help fill the vacuum of power resulting from the British withdrawal, the burden of the United States would be correspondingly lightened. Despite the reluctance of the United States to become involved in this region, a great power such as the United States cannot remain completely aloof.

While emphasizing foreign affairs, I have attempted to give due attention to internal developments because domestic affairs often affect foreign policy. The Iranian people have a great and glorious heritage. However, Iran like other Islamic countries went through a period of decline after the 17th century. The ineffectual leadership of the Qajar dynasty during the 19th and early 20th centuries was unable to cope with the dual threat of the Russians in the north and the British in India to the south, so that Iran was divided into spheres of influence by the so-called 1907 "partition of Persia." A constitutional movement at this time was only partially successful. Iran, although neutral in the First World War, was overrun by the belligerent powers. But a great leader arose to save the Iranian homeland in the person of Reza Shah Pavlavi, the Great, who consolidated Iran's strength and created basic institutions during 1925-1941. His son, Mohammad Reza Shah Pahlavi, was able to guide Iran safely through the Second World War on the side of the Allies. Despite political and economic problems in the post-war era, the Shah was able through firm leadership and good judgment to introduce policies which strengthened Iran's internal and external position. Thus, by 1967, American aid to Iran was phased out as the country recovered from economic difficulties.

Under the able leadership of the Shah, Iran's economy has grown at a rate of 10% a year in the last several years. The Iranian leadership has used the extensive oil revenues widely for economic and social development. Among the important developments in Iran during the last two decades have been the modernization of agriculture, land reform, and the establishment of new industries. New institutions have been developed to serve the nation such as the Literacy Corps or Education Corps (*Sepah-e Danesh*) in 1962, the Health Corps in 1964, and the Development Corps in 1965. Women have won the right to vote and now hold many important posts. A new middle class of business entrepreneurs and technocrats, as well as other professional groups, are now actively participating in the creation of a modern state.

Mohammad Reza Shah Pahlavi, Arya Mehr, who understands the needs and aspirations of the Iranian people, has in the last decade successfully led the nation so that political stability, economic growth, and social progress have become the order of the day. I therefore conclude that while the next decade may still be fraught with many difficulties, one can be more than cautiously optimistic about the outlook for Iran. The 1970's will be a period of even greater progress and accomplishment than the last decade.

13

I wish to express my thanks to Dr. Kerim Key for reading the manuscript and making useful suggestions, and take this opportunity to express my gratitude to the University of Tehran for making this study possible.

FIROUZ BAHRAMPOUR, Ph.D.
University of Tehran

Tehran, Iran

May 20, 1970

Introduction

THIS STUDY, which is an interpretation of modern Iranian history, is divided into nine short chapters. There is a brief foreword and preface. The main purpose of this essay is to introduce modern Iran and to assess the outlook for the future.

Chapter I is a survey of Iranian history. The cultural characteristics of Iranian civilization are summarized in Chapter II. Chapter III is devoted to the achievements of Reza Shah Pahlavi the Great, because he was the saviour of his country and is considered one of the great men of this century. Chapter IV deals with the accomplishments of Mohammad Reza Shah Pahlavi, Arya Mehr, who is determined to rule as a constitutional monarch but at the same time, being a wise and effective leader, who knows his countrymen well, is also determined to influence state affairs. He aims at leading the country in the right direction through progressive but workable reforms. This can only be done by the introduction of progressive legislation and at the same time by preventing extremist left-wing and right-wing elements from creating a chaotic situation. Chapter V is a brief essay on Iranian politics and government, not so much a description of the structure and political dynamics, as an analysis of the workings of the present Iranian system of government in actual practice. A brief statement on the new trends in the social life and organization of Iran is presented in Chapter VI. Chapter VII deals

15

with the problems of economic development, a subject vital to the future of the country. Iran's role in the world today is analyzed in Chapter VIII, while Chapter IX is a conclusion.

The selected bibliography is intentionally brief since the older standard works are already available in most bibliographies. An appendix containing H.I.M. the Shahanshah's address on the occasion of the Iranian New Year (March 21, 1970), a chronology of historical events, information on modern Iranian historiography, and the full text of the Iranian Constitution concludes this study.

CHAPTER I

Historical Heritage

THE HISTORY of Iran is divided into a number of historical periods.[1] Iranian history has had its periods of greatness and periods of stagnation and weakness. The periods of greatness and cultural flowering consist of four major peaks. They include the Achaemenid period (546 B.C.—330); the Sassanid period (226 A.D.-651); the Safavid period (1502-1736); and the Pahlavi era (1925 to the present time).

The Achaemenid period, which lasted from the 6th century to the 4th century B.C., is considered a time of great splendor, when the first "World State" was formed by the Iranian people. The Achaemenids ruled over a great empire which included divers people. They were tolerant in religious matters, and it will be remembered that it was Cyrus who liberated the Jews from the Babylonian captivity. The Achaemenians were also good administrators. The central government controlled the diverse provinces through the system of satrapies. A postal system of rapid couriers were used in order to communicate with the far-flung provinces of the empire. A just taxation system and coinage on a wide scale favorably affected the economy of the empire. The beginnings of Zoroastrianism are traced to this period. This great religion improved the ethical standards and influenced other religions. Effective administration of the bureaucracy, and a policy of tolerance, created a climate favorable for the process of fusing the Iranian and other peoples of the empire into a unified culture.

17

After a period of lesser rulers, the impact of Alexander the Great (331-329 B.C.), and the subsequent influence of Hellenism brought a new dimension into the Persian realms. However, this influence was of limited value and not permanent.

Another important era in the history of the Iranian people is the Sassanid period (226 A.D.-651). The period from 130 B.C. to 641 A.D., has been described as one of "East versus West" confrontation. The Parthian-Roman and the Sassanian-Byzantine rivalry resulted in a weakening of both East and West. Despite these struggles, the Sassanians were able to establish a centralized state, and the splendor of Iran emerged once again to bring the light of civilization to the world. Although its beginnings are traced to earlier times, it was during the Sassanian period that Zoroastrianism flourished. Iranian histories consider the Sassanians as the last native dynasty before the Arab-Muslim conquest. Present-day Iranians are proud of the Sassanian heritage. The present dynasty took the name Pahlavi from the Middle Persian language of Sessanian Iran. Today Sassanian motifs in art and architecture are popular and historical writers never tire in praising the glories of the Sassanian period. This, in a way, shows the continuity of Iranian culture.

The long wars wore out both the Byzantines and the Persians. The vacuum of power that was created was filled by the newly-emergent Arabs, whose Islamic religious zeal carried them forward from one conquest to the other. Thus, in the 7th century A.D., the Arabs brought Islam to Iran. Some Iranian historians claim that the Arab conquest had a negative influence on Iranian development. Actually, the Iranians were able to transform Islam to fit their own traditions and temperament. It will be remembered that the governmental organization of the Sassanians was not replaced and the Pahlavi language was used for several generations after the conquest. In the meantime, Arabic had become a universal language and rivalled Latin in the Middle Ages. The Iranians contributed significantly to the success of the Arabic language, for many Iranians wrote in Arabic during this period. The great grammarian of Arabic, Sibawaih was an Iranian. The great historian al-Tabari was an Iranian although he wrote his famous Chronicle of Apostles and Kings in Arabic. Others include Avicenna, al-Biruni, Rhazes, and al-Ghazalli to mention a few of the great men of the past.

The period from the 10th to the 13th century saw the Turkish-Mongol invasions from Central Asia. While the Turks became part of the now well-established Islamic civilization and contributed to the history of Iran, the Mongols created nothing but destruction and their contribution was largely negative.

The next peak in the history of Iranian history is reached during the 16th to 18th centuries when the Golden Age of the Safavids resulted in a new flowering of Iranian culture. This was also a period of struggle between the Iranian and Ottoman-Turkish Empires. The climax was reached at the Battle of Chaldiran in 1514, when Shi'ite Iran led by Shah Ismail Safavi met the Sunnite Ottoman Empire led by Sultan Selim in battle.

Shah Ismail Safavi (1502-1524) rose to power after a period of stagnation in Iranian history. The creation of a new Iranian dynasty under Shah Ismail was received with great enthusiasm by the people of Iran. The new Shah was able to unite the nation and restored the great Iranian traditions of the past. Shah Ismail was a pious Shi'ite, an excellent soldier, and a fine administrator. On the other hand, his adversary, Sultan Selim of the Ottoman Empire was an excellent soldier and a devout Sunnite, and the two leaders of the rival empires clashed as they struggled for the control of the Middle East. Shah Ismail was wounded in the thick of battle. This gave an advantage to the Ottomans but they did not pursue their victory. A stalemate developed in Iranian-Ottoman relations when Sultan Selim withdrew from the area to prepare an attack on the Mamelukes of Egypt. Shah Ismail died in 1524 and a period of weakness developed as a result of lesser rulers.

Again, after a period of chaotic conditions, a new ruler arose in the person of Shah Abbas the Great (1587-1629), who restored the glories of Iran. He struggled to consolidate his rule and unify the land. Shah Abbas was the greatest of the Safavids. He was brilliant in war, but also enjoyed the arts of peace. He stabilized the frontiers in the northeast against the Uzbegs, who had threatened Khorasan, and he captured Meshed. In 1624, he seized Baghdad from the Ottomans and a period of peace followed with the Ottoman Turks. After having secured the frontiers of Iran, he encouraged the arts, including miniatures, paintings, carpet-making, and architecture which flourished during this time. In 1598 Isfahan became the capital and was renowned for its splendor and beauty. "Isfahan is half the world" is even true today.[2] Shah Abbas the Great's reign lasted 42 years. Iran was respected in the world and foreign ambassadors arrived at the Safavid court in Isfahan to present their homage.[3] But after his death a period of weakness followed, when in 1722, Isfahan was captured by an Afghan army.

History again repeated itself. After a decade of troubled times, a new leader emerged to restore the prestige of Iran. Nadir Shah (1736-1747) was a leader of the Afshar tribesmen and a great military genius.[4] He has been compared to Napoleon because of his gift of swift movement and decisive action. In 1736, crowned as Nadir Shah (instead of a Safavid prince), he soon cleared Iran of its enemies. He was not content with restoring the Safavid boundaries, but extended the frontiers of Iran. In 1739 he invaded India, where he captured the Koh-i-Nor diamond. His armies entered Bokhara and Samarkand, and he made advances into the Caucasus to halt the Georgians and Russians. He conquered Mesopotamia and was a threat to the eastern portions of the Ottoman Empire. Despite his great military achievements, his contributions were not lasting. The great expenses involved in fighting wars left Iran in a weak condition after a brilliant reign of twelve years.[5] His empire broke apart soon after his death in 1747. There followed a period of lesser kings, the Zands (1750-1791).

The next stage in the history of Iran was the rise of the Qajar dynasty (1795-1923). This period was one of decline, especially after the first quarter of the 19th century, when the European powers began interferring in the internal affairs of Iran. The Pahlavi dynasty was to change all this after 1925.[6]

This writer concludes from his examination of the broad outlines of Iranian history that there were three great periods in the history of the Iranian people known to the world. These were the Achaemenid, the Sassanid, and the Safavid eras in which Iranian culture flourished. Great and lasting contributions were made in the fields of administration, the sciences, and religion, and the splendor of Iranian art, architecture, literature and poetry won renown for the Iranian people in the whole civilized world. In the past history of Iran, there were many invasions of diverse peoples. But they were all assimilated and became part of Iranian civilization. Also neighboring empires borrowed ideas and adopted Iranian institutions. There were, however, periods of stagnation and decline, the most recent being the Iran of the Qajars. The continuity of Iranian history and the inspiration derived from the glories of the past, give the Iranian people the confidence that is necessary to overcome calamities and strive again and again to achieve greatness. There is a new flowering of Iranian culture today which started with the advent of the Pahlavi Dynasty, and the emergence of Iran as a modern power in the Middle East can be considered a rebirth of this continuous cycle of the history of the Iranian people.

NOTES ON CHAPTER I

1. Iranian history has been divided into a number of periods shown below: Achaemenid dynasty, 546 B.C.-330; Seleucids, 320-262; Parthian period, 250 B.C.-226 A.D.; Sassanid dynasty, 226-651; Arab domina-

tion, 747-813; minor Persian dynasties, 820-1231; Ilkhanid and Timurid period, 1256-1500; Safavids, 1502-1736; Afsharids, 1736-1748; Zands, 1750-1794; Qajars, 1795-1923; Pahlavis, 1925 to present.

2. Isfahan nisf-i-jahan.

3. The reign of Shah Abbas the Great (1587-1629) coincided with that of Elizabeth of England, Akbar of India, and the rise of Muscovy in the north.

4. Nadir Shah was a Sunni.

5. Nadir Shas reminds one of Louis XIV of France who won many battles but weakened France financially.

6. The following works are useful sources for a study of the history of Iran: Richard N. Frye, *The Heritage of Persia,* New York, 1966; Joseph M. Upton, *The History of Modern Iran,* Cambridge, 1960; Donald N. Wilber, *Iran: Past and Present,* New York, 1948; Robert Payne, *The Splendor of Persia,* New York, 1957; and the *Cambridge History of Iran,* 1968.

CHAPTER II

Cultural Characteristics

THE CONTINUITY of Iranian culture is remarkable. The Iranians are a dynamic and resilient people with an illustrious historical heritage. Iran is known as the cradle of civilization. Iranians are proud of their Achaemenid, Sassanid, and Safavid dynasties. Iran is the land of art, history, and culture. Iran is great because the people of Iran are great. To outsiders this may sound an exaggeration, but to Iranians it is a cardinal belief. This is then, the first characteristic of Iranians, their great pride in their history, their great love for ther beautiful land, and their confidence in their destiny.

Iranians are somewhat mystical by nature. The great mystic poets of the past bear witness to this.[1] But they are also practical. Again, we can look to history to prove this contention. The Iranians of the Achaemenid and Sassanid periods were famous for their good government and administration.[2]

Iran's geographical position, as a bridge between East and West, affected the course of Iranian history. It gave Iranian civilization a distinct character—the ability to meet challenges through the capacity of assimilation. The various would-be conquerors were absorbed. While Iranians were able to keep alive their national tradition in face of foreign invasion, they were willing to adopt foreign ideas and customs. However, they usually improved on what they adopted.[3]

The Arab conquest of the 7th century A.D. was resisted effectively and Arabic Islam did not crush them, they merely improved on it through creative and imaginative actions, through mysticism, and through injection of beauty into the formalism of Islam. Exquisite Persian miniatures and pictures of saints, angels, and historical figures characterized Iranian art forms. The human form was not to be reproduced according to Arabic Islam, but the Iranians glorified the human form. Trees, flowers, animals all abound in Iranian art forms. Riding and hunting scenes were depicted in beautiful gay colors.

Iranians are deeply concerned with the purpose of life and are a truly religious people, but they are not dogmatic or narrow.[4] They have always been individualists. On the other hand, they have proven that they can move toward group cooperation and collective responsibility. Today Iranians must meet the requirements of modern times. Therefore, a new kind of education, new institutions, and methods of work are necessary. While this is true, it is also important to retain the basic elements of Iranian cultural tradition. The Shah is fully aware of this and is directing modernization within the framework of Iranian tradition and culture.

The continuity of Iranian culture is remarkable—this has been stressed in many works on Iran. This is true of their customs, language, literature, and art. Iranians are convinced that their traditions and culture will survive the greatest calamities and that they can surmount the greatest obstacles because it is their destiny to do so. This is because of their energy and resilience as well as their faith and optimism.

A major exhibition of Iranian art was held at the Metropolitan Museum of Art in New York in 1949.[5] The theme in 1964-5 was "7000 years of Iranian Art." This exhibition showed that Iranians have a great love for the arts. They also have a great love for their traditions. Iranians have resisted the influence of conquerors. Despite adversity that befell

24

them in the course of history, the Iranian people somehow always survived. In spite of the diversity of people who settled in Iran, the nation maintained its cultural unity. The culture of Iran moulded all newcomers into a nation. Iranians are filled with moral sentiments which can be seen in their proverbs, but their saving grace is their wonderful sense of humor. Iranian hospitality and love of things beautiful are well known. An imaginative and artistic people, Iranians did not take easily to dogma.

Space will only allow a few words about the Persian language, Iranian literature, and Iranian art.

Iranians are proud of their language. Language is one of the pillars of culture. Farsi (Persian) or the Iranian language is a member of the Indo-European family of languages. It belongs to the Aryan or Indo-Iranian branch of the family. The two ancient forms of Iranian are the old Persian language of the Achaemenids, and Avestan of the Zoroastrians. Ancient Persian is still studied in Iran and abroad. There is a direct continuity from Ancient Persian to Middle Persian languages of the Parthians and Sassanians. In fact, the prose and poetry of the 11th century can be understood today. Arabic words entered the language after the 7th century A.D., and provided the main distinction between Modern Persian and Middle Persian. Modern Persian is written in a modified Arabic script. The Persian script is more beautiful and graceful, Persian grammar is simple, and Persian is a harmonious language well suited to poetry.

Persian literature is admired the world over. The old poets of Iran are highly esteemed, even today. Most Persian poets are mystical and saturated with the love of God. Not only Iranians, but the whole world knows Firdausi, Jalal al-Din Rumi, Sadi, and Hafiz. In addition to poetry, the Persians wrote beautiful prose. During the Middle Ages, Persian was one of the great literary languages of the world. Only a few words will be possible on Persian writers and poets due to space limitations and this writer has chosen

Firdausi, Jalal al-Din Rumi, Sadi, and Hafiz, but there are hundreds of others who deserve attention.

Firdausi was an 11th century poet. He served in the court of Mahmud of Ghazna. He wrote epics of heroic legends of pre-Islamic Iran down to the Arab conquest. He praised the early Iranian heroes. His famous work is *Shahname* (Book of Kings).

Jalal al-Din Rumi (d. 1273) was a native of Balkh (Khorasan). His father settled in Konya during the Saljuq period, and Jalal al-Din Rumi grew up there. He wrote a *massnavi*, or didatic poem on the entire scope of mysticism of his day. He was an ecstatic poet who founded a religious order, the Mevlevi order of dervishes. His tomb is in Konya, Turkey, where he is revered not only by Persians and Turks but by the whole civilized world.

Sadi of Shiraz (d. 1291), was not only a poet but also a moralist and story-teller. He was the most travelled of the Persian poets. He rejoiced in life and hated injustice. His major work is *Gulistan* (Rose Garden).

Hafiz was the greatest of Persian lyric poets. He served in the court of Shiraz. He died in 1389.

It is in poetry that the Iranian faculty of pure abstraction finds its greatest expression. Even today, most educated Iranians quote poetry and compose their own lines since poetry is congenial to the Iranian temperament. Most Americans and Europeans know Omar Khayyam, although he is not among the greatest of Persian poets.[6]

For a history of Persian literature one can consult the admirable work of Edward G. Browne.[7] Today, many writers have found an outlet in newspapers, magazines and scholarly journals. Numerous books and biographies are published each year.

Iran was and still is a treasure house of the arts from which the Turks, Arabs and other nations drew in abundance. The design of Persian craftsmen were beautifully decorative. One authority has characterized the art of Iran as having ". . . precision, clarity, and lucidity."[8] Among the art forms that Iranians excelled in, one can mention carpets. The carpets of Kerman, Meshed, Kashan, Yezd, Bokhara, Shiraz, and Isfahan are famous the world over. Other art forms in which Iranians excelled are miniatures, architecture,[9] Persian gardens (gulistan), and Middle Eastern music. Other forms include pottery, bookbinding, metal work, wood inlay, and ceramics to mention a few.

Today, one can see the cradle of art and culture by visiting the museums of Tehran, Isfahan, Meshed, and Shiraz. For travelers interested in art, the Museums of Tehran (Musee Iran Bastan), the Museum of Gulistan Palace, the Museum of Antiquities in Isfahan, the Museum of the Shrine of Imam Reza in Meshed, and Pars Museum in Shiraz offer a really unique opportunity. Tehran Museum is a storehouse of the relics of Persian culture. Objects dated, 8000 years, sculpture from the Achaemenian era, metal work from the Sassanian period, as well as specimen of the arts of later times including the Saljuq, the Gaznevid, Ilkanid, and Safavid period can be found in the historic halls of this Museum. The Gulistan Palace Museum covers somewhat later periods and the Museums of Isfahan and Shiraz have fine collections of Persian art.

The best Persian miniatures are preserved at the Royal Library. Nothing can equal the fine Persian carpet as a piece of artistic work. Apart from the very precious samples in museums one can purchase beautiful carpets in the bazaars. Iran is the home of fine mosaic tilework seen in their splendor in Qum, Isfahan, and Meshed. Metal work, handmade silver and copper objects are now made in Isfahan and Shiraz. Filigree and embossed works in silver and brass are decorative in style and popular.

Besides the ancient ruins in Persepolis there are many fine mosques to admire. An example of Persian architecture is the famous Mosque in Isfahan. Beautiful tiles give this mosque a unique character.[10]

The cultural characteristics of the Iranian people, a most artistic and creative nation, is there for all to see in the ancient monuments and writings as well as in the more modern aspects of life which make Iran a country worth visiting and admiring.

NOTES ON CHAPTER II

1. For Sufism see A. J. Arberry, *Sufism*. London, 1950.
2. George G. Cameron, *History of Early Iran*. Chicago, 1936; A. T. Olmstead, *History of the Persian Empire*. New York, 1948; and R. Ghirsham, *l'Iran*, Paris, 1952.
3. Richard N. Frye, *The Heritage of Persia*. New York, 1963; Sir Percy Sykes, *A History of Persia*. London, 1930, 2 vols.; Donald N. Wilber, *Iran: Past and Present*. Princeton, 1948; Richard Payne, *The Splendor of Persia*. New York, 1957; and Firoze C. Davar, *Iran and Its Culture*. Bombay, 1953.
4. For a study of Iranian Islam see: Dwight M. Donaldson, *The Shi'ite Religion*. London, 1933.
5. *7000 Years of Iranian Art*. Washington, D. C., Smithsonian Publication 4535, 1965.
6. *Rubiyat of Omar Khayyam*. New York, Garden City Books, 1952.
7. See Edward G. Browne, *A History of Persian Literature*. Cambridge, 1924. See also A. J. Arberry, *Classical Persian Literature*. New York, 1958; R. Levy, *Persian Literature*. London, 1923; Hassan Kamshad, *Modern Persian Prose Literature*. Cambridge, 1966; Anne S. Mahdavi, *Persian Folk and Fairy Tales*. New York, 1966.
8. Donald N. Wilber, *op. cit.*, p. 90.
9. For Iranian art and architecture see: Andre Godard, *The Art of Iran*, New York, 1965; Arthur U. Pope, *Survey of Persian Art*. Oxford, 1938-39, 6 vols.; same author, *Persian Architecture*. London, 1965; Jane G. Mahler, *ed., Oriental Miniatures*. London, 1965; Basil Gray, *Persian Miniatures*, New York, 1964; same author, *Persian Painting*, New York, 1961; Hans E. Wulff, *The Traditional Crafts of Persia*, M.I.T. Press, 1966.
10. For Iranian cities see: Laurence Lockhart. *Famous Cities of Iran*. Brentford, Middlesex: Walter Pearce, 1939; Wilfred Blunt, *Isfahan: Pearl of Persia*. London: Elke Books, 1966.

CHAPTER III

Achievements of Reza Shah

REZA SHAH PAHLAVI the Great (1878-1944), Shah of Iran (1925-1941), was born in Alasht, province of Mazandaran, on March 16, 1878. The son of an Army officer, he joined the Army at an early age and rose rapidly from the ranks to the command of an Iranian Cossack brigade.[1]

Although attempting to remain neutral in the First World War, Iran was overrun by the belligerent powers, and the ineptitude of Ahmad Shah Qajar and his Ministers, reduced the country to a sad plight. In February 1921, Reza Khan gained control of the government, became Minister of War and Commander-in-Chief, and in 1923 Prime Minister. Since Ahmad Shah had left the country, Reza Khan became the Shah of Iran on December 16, 1925, and established the Pahlavi Dynasty. The Shah was known as a reformer. He ended brigandage, obtained control of the tribes, and made the authority of the central government effective throughout the land. He sponsored the construction of the Trans-Iranian Railway, which was completed in 1938 without foreign loans. The Trans-Iranian Railway is considered one of his great achievements. During his reign the road system was improved, industrial development was initiated, and basic institutions modelled on Western lines were established.[2]

Reza Shah was determined to modernize the industry of his country, but his past experience had made him suspicious of the Russians and the British. He therefore obtained machinery and technicians from Germany.

During 1941 British and Soviet pressure for the expulsion of German technicians working in Iran was rejected by Reza Shah as he considered this foreign interference as an infringement of Iranian sovereignty. As a result Anglo-Russian troops entered Iran, and Reza Shah abdicated in favor of his eldest son, who became Mohammad Reza Shah Pahlavi on September 17, 1941. The former Shah was exiled by the Allies first to Mauritius and later to South Africa, and he died in Johannesburg on July 26, 1944.

Considered the saviour of his country as was Mustafa Kemal Ataturk of Turkey, the Iranian people gave him the title Reza Shah Pahlavi the Great. His son, Mohammad Reza Shah Pahlavi has written a book about the achievements of his illustrious father, entitled "Reza Shah the Great."

In trying to establish a modern state, he had to contend with the opposition of extreme right-wing and left-wing elements. In order to carry out his program of reforms he had to use a firm hand in dealing with those who opposed his modernization reforms. Mustafa Kemal Ataturk had been faced with the same problems. Both Reza Shah and Ataturk have been criticized by some writers for being benevolent dictators. This is an unjust criticism. Both Reza Shah and Ataturk were only concerned with the welfare of the majority of the people of their respected countries.[3] Both had the overwhelming support of the people because they had saved their nations from foreign threats and domination and had brought justice, prosperity and prestige to their homelands.

NOTES ON CHAPTER III

1. His father died soon after his birth. Reza Khan showed exceptional aptitude and ability and rose from the ranks, was commissioned in the Iranian Army, and soon became a general and national hero.

2. For details of the modernization program of Reza Shah see: Amin Banai, *The Modernization of Iran, 1921-1941*. Palo Alto, 1962.
3. For Ataturk's policies and reforms see: Firouz Bahrampour, *Turkey: Political and Social Transformation*. New York: Theo. Gaus' Sons, 1967, Chapter II, Bernard Lewis, *The Emergence of Modern Turkey*, Oxford, 1961, Elaine D. Smith, *Turkey: Origins of the Kemalist Movement (1919-1923)*. Washington, D. C., 1959, Lord Kinross, *Ataturk*. New York, 1965.

CHAPTER IV

Achievements of Mohammad Reza Shah

H.I.M. MOHAMMAD REZA SHAH PAHLAVI, Shahinshah Ayra Mehr, was born in Tehran on October 26, 1919. He was proclaimed Crown Prince on April 24, 1925, and attended the Military School of Tehran during 1925-31. He completed his secondary studies in Switzerland in 1936, and graduated from the Military Academy of Iran in 1938. Commissioned in 1938, he was subsequently appointed Inspector of the Imperial Armed Forces. He ascended the 2500-year Iranian throne on September 17, 1941, after the abdication of his father, Reza Shah the Great, on September 16, 1941.[1]

Mohammad Reza Shah played an important role in the Tehran Conference during 1943, and he effectively safeguarded the interests of Iran. After leading his country through the perilous times of the Second World War on the side of the Allies, he was faced with a major crisis in 1945. The Shah was able during 1945-46, through firmness and astute diplomacy, to successfully resist Soviet threats in Azerbaijan. The United Nations was new at this time and the Iranian crisis was one of the first cases it had to handle. The Shah's courageous leadership finally resulted in the liberation of Azerbaijan by the Iranian Armed Forces.[2]

The early 1950's were a critical time in Iran. In 1950, the Shah inaugurated the first session of the Senate of Iran, and the following month, a Parliamentary bill to nationalize

32

the oil industry received his Royal Assent. In 1951, the Shah inaugurated an important land reform program. A royal decree resulted in the distribution of the Crown Lands to farmers. In order to promote effective utilization of the land distributed, the Shah ordered the establishment of a Development and Rural Cooperative Bank to furnish farmers with financial assistance, agricultural, and technical advice.

During the early 1950's, a political crisis developed, when Premier Mohammed Mossadegh (Premier during 1951-1953) followed ineffectual political and economic policies which created chaotic conditions.[3] The extreme left-wing Tudeh and the right-wing Fadayan-i-Islam also added to the tensions.[4] When the Shah dismissed Premier Mossadegh, he refused to accept dismissal and called on the Tehran mob to rise to his support, thus playing into the hands of the Tudeh.[5] However, the crisis was resolved when the people and the Armed Forces rallied to the support of the Shah, and General Fazollah Zahedi marched on Tehran on August 19, 1953, Dr. Mossadegh was arrested and order was restored. During this crisis the overwhelming majority of the Iranian people and political leaders backed the Shah.[6]

Immediately after the political stabilization of the country, the oil problem, which had brought the petroleum industry to a standstill, was resolved. The oil crisis had created serious economic and financial problems. Effective measures ended the economic crisis and oil revenues were restored. Since 1959, several new oil agreements have been negotiated with American and other foreign firms. These agreements established a new precedent in as much as they give Iran 75% of the profits.

In 1955, the Shah played a significant role in the formation of the Baghdad Pact, now known as CENTO.[7] The Shah's personal concern with foreign policy has strengthened the already close relations with the United States and the West, while through skillful diplomacy, he has been able to create a detente with the Soviet Bloc.

33

In his book *Mission for My Country*, the Shah set forth his plans for reform and modernization.[8] During the 1960's the Shah's program was successfully initiated as Iran's position in the international field was secure and internal conditions improved.

In 1963, the Shah launched his famous "White Revolution" following a national referendum, which gave overwhelming approval to his proposals for reform. The reform program consists of six principal points summarized here: 1) Land reform, 2) nationalization of forests, 3) change of government-owned factories into joint-stock companies, 4) a profit sharing scheme for factory workers, 5) amendment of the electoral law, and 6) creation of a Literary Corps to strengthen education in rural areas. Since that time additional reforms involve the formation of Health Corps, a Development Corps, as well as renovations in the administrative and academic fields.

The Shah has sought to expand his country's economy and improve the lot of the people through a number of economic development plans. That these plans have been successful is evidenced by a remarkable economic growth attained in the last few years amounting to 10% a year. In the meantime, cost-of-living increases have been slight, amounting to a little over 1.5% a year.[9]

Mohammad Reza Shah is a natural born leader. He is determined to rule as a constitutional monarch, but is also convinced that he has to direct the nation. The reactionary landlords and fanatical Mullahs resisted reforms and modernization as did the left-wing elements. His democratic temper has made possible the successful modernization of his country. The Shah possesses an instinctive knowledge of what is possible. He is pragmatic in his approach to political issues and is persistent in his efforts to improve the standard of living of the people.

The Shah is a skilled pilot and understands machines. He is aware of the importance of industrialization. At the same time, he is an expert farmer, and thus is close to the farmers and peasants. He favors the growth of a prosperous middle class and thus has the support of the business and industrial entrepreneurial classes as well as the new technocrats who are participating effectively in the development of the country. The Shah has good advisors and has followed policies that have proven successful. Most important, the Shah has an intimate knowledge of his own country and a sincere concern for the welfare of all the people. This has made it possible for him to mobilize the whole nation and move Iran forward. As one authority of Iranian affairs has so aptly put it, "the splendor of Ancient Persia is being revived"[10] under the leadership of Mohammad Reza Shah Pahlavi.

NOTES ON CHAPTER IV

1. The Shah postponed the coronation ceremonies for twenty-five years, because he was determined to improve the lot of his people and assure the stability of his country first. The Coronation of the Shah and Empress Farah took place on October 27, 1967. His Royal Highness Reza Pahlavi, the Crown Prince, was born on October 31, 1960. The *farman* proclaiming H.R.H. Prince Reza as Crown Prince was issued by His Imperial Majesty in November 1960. For details about the Royal Family and other leaders of Iran see: *Iran Almanac 1969,* published by Echo of Iran, Tehran, Iran, 1969, pp. 731-786.
2. Iran was invaded by Anglo-Russian forces on August 25, 1941. Reza Shah abdicated on September 16, 1941, and the next day his eldest son ascended the throne. See George Lenczowski, *Russia and the West in Iran.* Cornell University, 1949, and Richard Van Wagenen, *The Iranian Case 1946.* New York, Carnegie, 1952.
3. On February 4, 1949, during ceremonies commemorating the founding of the University of Tehran, an attempt was made on the Shah's life by a terrorist who fired five pistol shots at point blank range. Although wounded, the Shah miraculously survived.
4. The Tudeh (Masses) is an illegal pro-Communist party. The Fadayani-i-Islam (Martyrs of Islam) is an extreme right-wing group. In 1949, Dr. Mossadegh undertook the leadership of the National Front. He was Premier April 1951-June 1952, and July 1952-July 1953. After August 1953 the leadership of the National Front was split and it has lost support in the country.
5. See Joseph M. Upton, *The History of Modern Iran.* Cambridge, 1960, pp. 95-98.

6. After having resolved the political crisis in 1953, the Shah initiated a new era in his reign. Since that time, he has repeatedly declared that he is no longer only the hereditary but also the elected king of the country. See *Iran Almanac 1969, op. cit.,* p. 733.
7. See Chapter VIII for Iran's foreign relations.
8. H.I.M. Mohammed Reza Shah Pahlavi, Shahanshah of Iran, *Mission for My Country.* New York, 1961.
9. See Chapter VII for problems of economic development.
10. Robert Payne, *The Splendor of Persia.* New York, 1957, p. 232.

CHAPTER V

Government and Politics

IRAN IS A CONSTITUTIONAL MONARCHY headed by the Shah.[1] The Iranian Constitution upholds the rights of equality of individuals, security of their lives, property, homes, and honor. It also upholds the right to bring legal action in competent courts, the right of personal and social freedom of expression, freedom to write, freedom to assemble, and freedom of ownership. Foreign nationals living in Iran enjoy the same freedoms and rights as Iranians. All rights and freedoms are laid down in the Constitution.[2]

The Shah is the traditional head of the nation. The Prime Minister, or Head of Government, and the Cabinet are selected by the Shah, with the approval of both houses of parliament, and serves at his pleasure.

The bicameral legislature is composed of the *Majlis* or Lower House, and the Senate. The *Majlis* has 219 seats,[3] and Deputies are elected for four-year terms. The Senate consists of 60 members serving four-year terms, half of the Senate membership being appointed by the Shah, the other half being elected. Of the 30 elected members of the Senate, 15 Senators are elected from Tehran, and 15 from the provinces. Suffrage is universal for all Iranians over the age of twenty.

The last parliamentary elections were held in August 1967. The *Iran-e-Novin* Party (New Iran Party) won 183 seats out of 219 seats. The *Mardom* Party (People's Party) won 28, the Pan-Iranist Party won 5, and an Independent

37

won one seat in the *Majlis*. In the Senate, the New Iran Party had 48 seats, the Mardom Party 11 seats, and one seat was held by an Independent Senator.[4] The New Iran Party won the municipal elections held in October 1968. Members of the Mardom Party, the Pan-Iranist Party, and Independents were also elected.[5]

The legal system and the organization of the courts, based largely on the French and Belgian systems, has also drawn from other continental systems. The judicial system once entirely religious has been secularized. Personal law is still based on Islamic practice. While the courts are secularized, there is surveillance to insure that no law is contrary to the principles of the official Shiite Islam. There are courts from the small district level up to the highest court. There are commercial, criminal and civil courts. The judicial power lies within the jurisdiction of the courts of justice, and certain exclusive cases fall within the jurisdiction of special military courts. The High Court of Appeal may judge disputes relating to government departments.

Iran is divided into 14 *Ostans* or provinces, and 6 independent governorates, subdivided into counties, municipalities, and rural districts. The Governor-General and other officials are appointed by the Shah.

Since the key internal problem facing the country is economic development and modernization, an important aspect of the nation's political life is the alignment of diverse political elements in support of the Shah's reform program. The New Iran Party, founded after the 1963 elections, is the majority party in the parliament. Under the Shah's effective leadership and with the support of the New Iran Party, the Government is committed to an ambitious program of economic, social, and administrative reform, and the modernization of the country's defense forces.

Land reform is the most important of all the many-faceted reform program, and has attracted the greatest attention and publicity within and outside Iran. The land distribution was carried out in two major stages. After the completion of the land distribution program in 1962, the Government announced in 1966, a third stage which was concerned with comprehensive agricultural development. This included technical assistance for farmers, increased agricultural credit and support for rural cooperatives, marketing improvements, and expanded rural education and health.[6]

Emancipation of women has made remarkable progress, with women voting in the last parliamentary elections and a number being elected. Women have been appointed to high government posts, and participate in the educational and other fields of endeavor. Some of the other successful programs include the Literacy or Educational Corps; the Health Corps; and the Development Corps.

Significant efforts have been made to maintain the impetus behind the reform program. At the same time, an effort was made to develop new institutions to take the place of old ones which were affected by the land reform.

The above background of the reform policy of the Shah is presented in order that the political dynamics and the composition of the political parties is better understood. Political parties or groups are divided into two types. The legal political parties and those which are banned. The New Iran Party, the Mardom Party, and the Pan-Iranist Party are legal parties. The *Tudeh* (Masses) and the diverse elements which formed the National Front are no longer legal parties and have lost support in Iran.[7]

The purpose of this chapter is not to discuss the political dynamics or present a detailed history of the political parties. It merely presents sufficient background material in order to explain the reason for the present political system, and attempts to show how this system of government has led to political stability and progress.

A study of Iranian politics will show that Iran today has an effectively operating system of government in which responsible parties and political leaders cooperate in the social and economic development of the country.

In addition to the responsible parties, there are a number of parties or groupings of the extreme right and left which are banned. Of these, the leftists are potentially more harmful to the Iranian destiny. While the leftist parties and individuals are no longer active in Iran, where they have no support, they operate abroad. Some of their leaders issue left-wing papers and indulge in anti-government activities. They are now split into pro-Soviet and pro-Peking factions.

A brief survey of political parties is presented here before discussing the present parties and their programs. One can divide the history of political parties into two major periods, 1905 to 1963, and since 1963. Also the period from 1905 to 1963 can be divided into a number of periods, in which, certain developments affected the growth of Iranian political parties.

The Persian Revolution and Constitutional Period lasted from 1905 to 1921.[8] This was followed by the Reformist Period under Reza Shah Pahlavi the Great (1923-1941), when basic institutions were established. The period 1941 to 1946, the war years and the immediate aftermath, saw the beginnings of some embryonic political parties or groupings. The Soviets backed the Tudeh, which was opposed by Seyyid Zia Tabatabai and the National Will Party, and Ahmad Qavam's Democrat Iran Party. However, the Tudeh was banned after the withdrawal of the Soviets from Northern Iran, and the Tabatabai and Qavam parties failed to gain sufficient support. The period 1946-1950 was characterized by the appearance of a number of splinter groups which tried to organize political parties. Some of the leaders of these groupings later joined the newly-emerging parties. During this period the beginnings of the Iran Party, the Mardom Iran Party, the Pan-Iranist Party, the Toilers Party, and the Fadayan-i-Islam and others are to be seen.[9] Although outlawed, the Tudeh continued to agitate whenever the opportunity arose.

During 1950-1953, the National Front, which was led by Dr. Mohammed Mossadegh since 1949, attempted unsuccessfully to unify the diverse elements into a political force. Mossadegh was Prime Minister during 1951-1953. His policies led to a political crisis, and when he played into the hands of the Tudeh, he was overthrown in August 1953 by General Zahedi and the supporters of the Shah.[10] The period 1953-1957 was one of readjustment and political activity was limited. Zahedi was Prime Minister from August 1953 to April 1955, when he resigned on grounds of ill-health. He was succeeded by Hossein Ala, who was followed by Manuchehr Eqbal. In the meantime, the Shah, desirous to strengthen parliamentary democracy, encouraged the development of a two-party system in the Majlis. Thus, during 1958 and 1959 the *Melliyun* Party (Government Party), led by Dr. Eqbal and the Mardom Party (People's Party) led by Assadollah Alam emerged and tried to develop a two-party system by cooperating with each other. However, these parties were unable to function effectively, and when in 1960 elections were held, it was alleged that the elections were rigged and they were declared null and void. Prime Minister Dr. Eqbal resigned. In the winter of 1960, a second attempt at elections were again unsuccessful. In both the 1960 elections the National Front, led by Allahyar Saleh from Kashan, was permitted to participate. The parties participating were the Mardom, Melliyun and National Front. Again election irregularities prevented the proper functioning of political parties. Engineer Jafar Sherif-Emami of the Mardom was chosen Prime Minister, but his Government lasted only a few months. The Shah then appointed Dr. Ali Amini, an economist and independent to form a government in order to solve the serious economic problems facing the nation. Dr. Amini imposed austerity measures and tried to obtain budgetary aid from the United States. His failure to obtain this aid further weakened his position, and his Cabinet which lasted from April 1961 to July 1962, came to an end with the appointment of Assadollah Alam of the Mardom Party to the Premiership.

After discussing briefly the earlier political developments

41

and the role of political groups, the more recent developments which can be said to have started during 1962-1963
will be presented below.

During 1962-1963 three important political events took
place that are worth noting. The National Front held a
Congress during December 1962 and tried to challenge the
Government. However, the Front was badly split and despite its violent invectives it was not successful in its aims.
To counter the National Front, and to gain support for his
reform program, the Shah called for a Peasants' Congress
in order to initiate their participation in the political life
of the country. The Peasant Delegates were organized
throughout Iran. The Shah's Referendum on January 26,
1963 followed, in which he received an overwhelming support of 5,593,826 votes in favor of his six-point reform program, now officially called the "White Revolution." As a
result, the *Iran-e-Novin* Party, sometimes referred to as the
Iran *Novin* Party (New Iran Party) was organized in 1963
out of the "Progressive Center," by Hassan Ali Mansur, who
became Premier in 1964. Mansur was chosen to carry out
the reform program, but he was assassinated in January
1965. Amir Abbas Hoveyda, a most able leader replaced
him as Prime Minister. The New Party won the 1967
elections and as the majority party, is implementing the
"White Revolution." The Party opposes "feudalism" and
favors following an independent national policy.[11]

The Mardom Party is the minority party. It was founded
in 1957 by Mr. Assadollah Alam. The Mardom participated
in the two elections of 1960, which were annulled because
of alleged collusion between the Mardom and the Mellyun
majority party. When the *Majlis* was dissolved, Mr. Alam
resigned from the leadership of the Mardom. In 1963, a
group of Mardom members left the Party to join the New
Iran Party. This weakened the Mardom Party. However,
the Mardom has been able to hold together a number of
deputies in the *Majlis*, and has played the role of a minority

party. After Mr. Alam's resignation, Senator Professor Yahya Adl took over the post of Party Secretary-General.[12]

The Pan-Iranist Party is a nationalistic party which favored the annexation of Bahrain.[13] It has only 5 seats in the Majlis. It is an anti-Communist party.[14]

A few words on the National Front and the Tudeh parties will conclude this discussion. The National Front was never a real party, but a coalition of diverse neutralist and urban elements. The National Front was discredited because it opposed the reform program of the Shah.[15]

The Tudeh Party is banned today. The Tudeh, which is a Communist Party, can trace its origins to the first Iranian Communist Party formed in 1920. The Communists have tried unsuccessfully to disrupt Iranian society and gain control with outside aid during such periods as 1920-1921, 1945-1946, and 1951-1953. The Tudeh Party itself was formed in October 1941 and was led by the late Soleiman Mohsen Eskandari. During 1941-1945, the Tudeh's main aim was to be an anti-Fascist force. In 1944, the Tudeh gained 8 seats in the Majlis. During the 1945-1946 Azerbajian crisis the Tudeh sided with outside forces. In 1949, 3 members became Ministers in the Qavam Cabinet. Although outlawed in 1949, it continued to be active, and in the early 1950's it sought the cooperation of the rightists.[16] After the downfall of the Mossadegh Cabinet, the Government closed all Tudeh organizations in Iran. Tudeh leaders escaped to East Berlin and Eastern European countries, where they continue their activities.

The Tudeh program calls for the overthrow of the government, withdrawal from CENTO, and renationalization of the oil industry. The Tudeh is continuing its efforts to create a united front of anti-imperialist forces, and operates a radio station believed to be located in East Germany. It issues anti-government and pro-Communist propaganda publications but has no influence in Iran today.

The Iranian political system is based on a Western type of Constitution but is adapted to the special requirements of the nation arising from its geographical location and its historical traditions. Iranian political organization is in transition and political parties in the modern sense are new.[17]

As seen from a discussion of the political parties above, tolerance of disruptive elements, have in the past threatened the security and independence of Iran. Also, in Iran, the monarchy has been traditionally popular with the majority of the people. Left-wing elements who are small in numbers and who agitated against the monarchy on several occasions, soon found out that they were not acceptable to the majority of Iranians who are nationalistic and loyal to their traditions. The main opposition to the Shah's reform program has come from reactionary mullahs and leftist extremists.

The Iranian leadership of today is trying through evolutionary methods to broaden participation in national affairs. New democratic-type institutions are being developed and the nation is fully mobilized to work for the modernization of their country.[18]

After surveying in broad strokes the history of political parties, this writer will in the following paragraphs attempt to summarize his views on the political system of Iran as it has evolved in the course of the last decade.

In the preceding pages, it has been shown that there are a number of Iranian political parties dedicated to the development of a strong and free Iran. Individual political leaders and political groups will play an important role and have their following. The existing political system which is in transition, and which is constantly adapting itself to new requrements, appears to be working effectively, especially in the last decade. Nationalism is a positive force in Iran and the Shah's dynamic social and economic policies have won him the support of the majority of the nation. The whole nation is motivated by patriotism and the desire to remain independent. Therefore, most Iranians are convinced that it would be a mistake to allow parties such as the Tudeh, and other radical groups, freedom of action. Experience has shown that these radical elements tend to disrupt the peaceful and orderly development of the country.

Today, there is freedom of speech and press in Iran, within the limitations of existing Constitutional laws and regulations. There are political parties and local and national elections. However, irresponsibility and anarchy will not be tolerated. This would end the orderly social and economic development and jeopardize the many gains achieved in the last decade.

From time to time, foreign critics of the Iranian Government, misled by radical propaganda, will misrepresent existing conditions. As far as the majority of the Iranian people are concerned, only legitimate political parties which support the Constitution and favor national unity and independence are to be tolerated. These views have been expressed in a number of national elections and referendums. It is the view of this writer that extremist radical groups who advocate the overthrow of the government and the destruction of the Constitution are rightly banned. The Iranian leaders backed by the overwhelming majority of the people will not allow the destruction of the nation by disloyal, disruptive, or misguided elements whose main support is derived from outside foreign sources.

NOTES ON CHAPTER V

1. The Shah is the traditional leader of the Iranian people, and the 2500-year old monarchy is popular. See E. A. Bayne, *Persian Kingship in Tradition*. N. H. Hanover: American Universities Field Service Staff, 1968, and Robert Payne, *The Splendor of Persia*. New York, 1957.
2. See Appendix for the complete text of the Iranian Constitution with amendments.
3. The *Majlis* has 219 seats, with 2 vacant seats for islands of the Persian Gulf.
4. For information on political parties and national and municipal elections see: *Iran Almanac 1969*. Tehran: Echo of Iran, 1969, pp. 148-151.

5. *Ibid.,* p. 152.
6. See Chapters VI and VII for details on social and economic problems.
7. The *Iran Almanac 1969, op. cit.,* lists the following parties which were active in recent years and which have ceased their activities or have merged with other groups. Afro-Asian Group (1961-1963), Association of Friends (1963-1964), Defenders of the Constitution (1962-1963), Fadayan-i-Islam (1964-1965), Guardians of Freedom (inactive since 1963), the Islamic Nations' Party (1964-1965), Melliyun Party (1957-1963), and Progressive Party (inactive since 1965). For names of political leaders and further details see: *op. cit.,* p. 148.
8. Edward G. Browne, *The Persian Revolution of 1905-1909.* Cambridge University, 1910.
9. In June 1950 Ali Razmara was appointed as a reformist Prime Minister, and the future looked bright. However, he was assassinated on March 7, 1951 by a member of the Fadayan-i-Islam, and on April 27, 1951 Hossein Ala, who had followed Razmara as Prime Minister resigned. Mossadegh was Premier April 1951 to June 1952, and July 1952 to July 1953. Overthrown August 19, 1953.
10. General Fazlollah Zahedi won fame when he marched on Tehran on August 19, 1953 in support of the Shah during a political crisis resulting from Premier Mossadegh's refusal to be dismissed by the Shah. For a brief biography of General Zahedi, Dr. Mossadegh and other leaders see: Mehdi Heravi, *ed., Encyclopedia of the Middle East.* Washington, D. C., Public Affairs Press, 1971.
11. During 1968-1969, the Imperial Inspectorate discovered some irregularities and several members of the New Iran Party were relieved from membership in the Party. This indicates that the Iranian leadership is insistent in having honest and efficient government. See *Iran Almanac 1969, op. cit.,* p. 153.
12. *Iran Almanac 1969, op. cit.,* pp. 150-153.
13. The Pan-Iranist Party has recently agreed to cooperate with the Government in trying to solve problems involving the Persian Gulf on a non-partisan basis.
14. *Iran Almanac 1969, op. cit.,* p. 154.
15. In 1949, Dr. Mossadegh assumed leadership of the National Front and favored nationalization of the oil industry. The first phase of the National Front's existence lasted from 1949 to 1953. With the downfall of Mossadegh in 1953, the party split, some of its supporters were imprisoned and others left for foreign countries where they continued their activities with little effect. The second phase of the National Front's activities started in 1963, when the Front participated in demonstrations and issued anti-government leaflets. The authorities cracked down on them in 1965, and arrested Khalil Maleki of the Socialist League (left-wing faction of the National Front). He was pardoned and removed himself from politics. After 1965 the Front's activities were shifted to Europe. Dr. Mossadegh died at the age of 86, on March 5, 1967.
16. The extreme right led by the late Ayatollah Kashani and his Fadayan-i-Islam, although anti-Communist, cooperated with the Tudeh in 1952

in anti-British demonstrations. Mossadegh made the mistake of seeking the support of the Fadayan as well as the Tudeh. Kashani died on March 14, 1962.

17. For a discussion of the *dowreh*, the decline of the Bazaar, and the rise of political parties see: William G. Miller, "Political Organization in Iran: From Dowreh to Political Party," *Middle East Journal*, Spring and Summer 1969.

18. Principal Iranian Government Officials: Monarch—The Shahanshah, His Imperial Majesty Mohammad Reza Shah; Prime Minister—Amir Abbas Hoveyda; Chief of the Supreme Commander's Staff—General Feridun Djam; Foreign Minister—Ardeshir Zahedi; Finance Minister —Jamshid Amuzegar; Director of the Plan Organization—Mehdi Samii; Ambassador to the U.S.—Amir Aslan Afshar; Ambassador to the U.N.—Mehdi Vakil. Note: During 1970 Dr. Khodadad Farman-farmaian was appointed Director of the Plan Organization, and Dr. Mehdi Samii became Governor of the Central Bank of Iran.

CHAPTER VI

Social Life and Organization

A BRIEF SURVEY of the Iranian establishment and the emerging structure of modern Iranian society will be presented here. In the past, Iran was an Islamic Empire.[1] During the zenith of Islamic greatness, Iranian society was prosperous and brilliant in its achievements.[2] But a period of stagnation followed, when little progress took place in the social field as in other areas of Iranian life. Thus, at the dawn of the 20th century, Iran was still virtually a feudal state.

When Reza Shah the Great took over the reins of government in 1925, Iranian society consisted of the ruling elites, the bureaucrats, the landlords, the Army, and the *mullahs*. The peasantry was depressed, and the tribes were unruly. The middle class was small, consisting primarily of merchants and traders in the bazaar. There was virtually no industry in the modern sense of the word, or a trained industrial labor force. Iranian society was decentralized, the Central Government had little control over the country, and there was a lack of national purpose and unity.

Reza Shah tried to modernize Iran during his reign (1925-1941). He was able to strengthen the Central Government, establish new institutions, and create the necessary climate for the growth of patriotism and national unity.[3]

In the following pages, a brief discussion of the social developments as they affected the life of peasants, urban dwellers, and tribal elements will be presented to help the

48

reader assess the social changes that took place in the last few decades.

The peasants and farmers lived at a subsistence level. They were attacked by brigands and tribal elements, and were at the mercy of the landlord. During the reign of Reza Shah, brigandage was ended, tribes were brought under control, and the *kadkhuda* (village headman) became responsible for the good government of the village. Despite the poverty of the peasants, Communist propaganda among them failed, because the peasants were devout Muslims and had a great love for their traditions and the soil on which they worked. Today, the Iranian peasant is industrious, hardy, religious, and patriotic.

The peasantry, or what we can today call the farmers and rural population, is an important base on which Iranian society is built. The peasantry supports the monarchy. Reza Shah was admired by the peasantry because he freed them from the attacks of brigands and tribesmen. In the mind of the peasantry, Reza Shah was a strong and benevolent leader in the tradition of the great legendary heroes of the glorious past.

In the same way, Mohammad Reza Shah has the admiration of the peasants. His land reform program has endeared him to the peasants whose economic and social position has been improved during the last decade. The power of the landlords has been finally broken. Also, the Education Corps, the Development Corps, and the Health Corps have helped in the rural areas and their impact has been significant. Institutions now exist to help the farmers both economically and socially. This involves credit to farmers, technical assistance, and social insurance.

While Reza Shah was able to limit the power of the *mullahs* and *sayyids*, who were powerful in rural areas as well as in the cities, it was only in recent years that the strength of fanatical religious elements, who opposed reforms, was finally curtailed. Thus, Mohammad Reza Shah was able through great courage and skill to end the power of both the landlord class and religious reactionaries.[4]

The modernization program was started in the cities and towns. While most Iranians live in the rural areas,[5] the urban population is more dynamic and mobile and plays an important role in the life of the nation. The Iranian urban population is growing with industrialization. There is a flow of peasants from the rural areas into the cities in search of jobs. The importance of the Bazaar, the center of commercial life in the larger cities, is gradually declining with the growth of a modern commercial and industrial entrepreneurial class and the rise of the new professional groups and technocrats. The emancipation of women has made possible the more effective use of population resources in a developing society. The newly-emerging middle class strongly supports the Shah's modernization program and participates fully in the development of the country.

Another group making up the social structure of Iran is the nomadic and semi-nomadic tribes. As mentioned before, the Central Government had little control over the tribes in the past. However, during the reign of Reza Shah the tribes were brought under control, many were settled in agricultural communities, and most of them have been integrated into the mainstream of the life of the nation. The principal tribes totalling about 3 million, are now supporters of the Government. The main tribal groups include the Kurds in the northwest, the Qashqais and Bakhtiaris in the southwest, and smaller groups such as the Lurs, Baluchis, and others.

Having examined briefly the three main subdivisions of the population, several other aspects of Iranian life will be discussed. While trying to avoid too much detail, a few words regarding the composition of the Iranian population is deemed necessary.

Historically, the majority of Iranians are Shiite Muslims, with a small number of Sunnite Muslims and others making up the population. Today, 93% of the people are Shiites,

5% Sunnites, and 2% other (including Zoroastrians, Christians, and Jews).[6]

Roughly 45% of the employed population is engaged in agriculture, 18% in manufacturing, 18% in services, 8% in commerce, 8% in construction, and 5% in other activities (including transportation, communication, sanitation, and mining).

Social changes have been more rapid in the urban areas, where schools and universities,[7] modern dwellings and buildings, and new services have grown in the last two decades. While progress has been slower in rural areas, a concentrated effort is being made to improve the lot of the rural population, and the "White Revolution" reforms include uplift of the economic and social level of the peasantry, the urban workers,[8] and the whole population. Also, great strides have been taken in the development of social welfare and insurance.[9]

Iranian society is in a transitional period. In the past, social life was feudal in nature. The *mullahs* played an important role in the life of the nation. The landlords enjoyed a good life, but the peasantry and the urban workers were ignorant and poor. Constant wars and internal upheavals prevented the development of a dynamic and progressive society. Today, all that has changed as a result of good government and a period of peace.

One may observe the changes in Iranian society by selecting a number of indicators. In the past, people did not vote and had no voice in the government. Today the peasant as well as the city dweller have the vote. Women now participate in every field of endeavor whereas in the past they were limited in their activities and wore a veil. Perhaps, one indicator is dress. Whereas traditional dress is still worn in the rural areas, and on festive occasions by cultural groups, most Iranians today have adopted the Western style of dress.

Another indicator is the decline of the old bazaar, which was the center of commercial activity in the larger cities.

51

The bazaari employed workers, were allied closely with the *mullahs,* and often was involved in political activities and rumors, generally resisting modernization and change. The bazaari is being replaced by owners of new commercial and industrial enterprises. The new bureaucrats, technocrats, and intellectuals, and trained workers are replacing the old bazaari and his apprentices and workers. Two centers of social life in the bazaar is the *chai khaneh* (teahouses) and *zurkhaneh* (traditional houses of strength, or gyms). Praying at the mosque and pilgrimages to holy shrines are also considered social functions. Today, the traditional teahouses are still filled with workers who have perhaps recently migrated from the villages for jobs in the city. But, on the other side of town, one may see modern banks, hospitals, hotels, restaurants, theaters, and movies springing up, often replacing the old buildings and institutions. For example, the old *zurkhanehs* are being replaced by modern tennis courts, bowling alleys, and athletic fields. The tourist is still charmed by the old fruit and vegetable markets, but supermarkets are now appearing in the bigger cities and towns.

Iranians like to go on picnics, they visit relatives in town or in other parts of the country, and there is an active social life in Tehran. To the tourist, Iran's chief attraction is its wealth of historical sites, notably in Tehran, Isfahan, Rasht, Tabriz, Susa, Persepolis, and its museums of Persian art and culture. Tourism is under the care of the Iranian Tourist Organization in Tehran, where there are many museums and historical sites.

Iran has many new schools and universities. Literacy of the population over ten years of age and over was 28.1% according to the 1966 census. Literacy is 49.1% in urban areas and 13.7% in rural areas. Nearly 2.5 million pupils are enrolled in primary schools, and secondary school enrollment reached nearly 700,000. University students increased from about 30,000 students in 1968 to 36,000 in 1969. There are eight universities in Iran today.[10]

Iranian labor has made great strides both as to working

conditions and wages, as well as training and social insurance. The labor force is estimated at about 8 million, of which about half are engaged in agriculture, and about 20% in industry. There is a shortage of skilled labor and great efforts have been made in training the labor force. The Labor Law of 1959 is the basic labor legislation. The Workers' Social Insurance Act of 1960 insures workers and provides the usual benefits. Under the Profit Sharing Act of 1963, workers in industrial and manufacturing enterprises are entitled to share up to 20% of the net profits. Labor syndicates and unions are permitted by the Iranian Labor Law. The largest syndicates are those in the petroleum industry. Iran is a member of the International Labor Organization and has representation in the International Confederation of Free Trade Unions.[11]

Social welfare has always been part of Islamic society, but today the old Islamic institutions are being gradually replaced by Western type of social welfare organizations. The Pahlavi Foundation established in 1958, has received considerable gifts from the Shah for improving the education, health, and social welfare of the poorer citizens. National service draftees with medical experience have been formed into a Health Corps, bringing medical assistance to outlying areas of the country. The Fourth Development Plan provides for 14,000 new hospital beds.[12]

Social insurance is new but important. It involves not only government employees, workers, and farmers, but nearly all segments of society. There are also charitable organizations, and endowments. The Iranian equivalent of the Red Cross is the Red Lion and Sun Society of Iran. The Farah Pahlavi Charity Foundation was organized in 1963 to help orphans and children. There are many other organizations, but only a few examples are given here.[13]

This brief survey of social development in Iran indicates that the outlook for the future is bright. While modernization involves changes in the structure of Iranian society, the Iranian leadership is aware that superficial copying of the

West is not sufficient to create a viable society. Therefore, while adopting new institutions, an effort is being made to relate Western institutions and methodology to the Iranian tradition and thus establish a national culture with deep roots in the past, but geared for survival and further growth in the modern world. The best of Iranian tradition is to be retained, and the best that the West has to offer is to be adopted.[14]

NOTES ON CHAPTER VI

1. Iranian historians will also stress that Iranian institutions and civilization can be traced beyond the Islamic past to the greatness of Ancient Iran.
2. Ann K. Lambton, *Islamic Society in Persia.* London University, 1954. See also: Richard N. Frye, *ed., Islam and the West.* The Hague: Mouton, 1957; C. T. Young, *ed., Near East Culture and Society.* Princeton, 1951; Sydney N. Fisher, *ed., Social Forces in the Middle East.* Ithaca, Cornell, 1955; and Kemal H. Karpat, *ed., Political and Social Thought in the Middle East.* New York, Praeger, 1968 (Part III, Political and Social Thought in Iran, pp. 373-390).
3. The building of railroads and roads, the development of industrial, financial, and educational institutions, and the settlement of some nomadic tribes all helped in modernizing Iran. Also, national pride was strengthened by his effective foreign policies. See Chapter III for the Achievements of Reza Shah Pahlavi.
4. Iranians are religious people, and there is religious freedom and respect and tolerance for all religions. However, fanatical elements who opposed reforms and obstruct progress could not be allowed to slow down the modernization of the nation.
5. Iran's population in the last census, held in 1966, was 25,781,000, of which 15.3 million was rural, 9.8 million urban, and 0.6 million nomadic. The annual rate of population growth is about 3% and the 1970 estimated population is nearly 29 million. The area of Iran is 628,000 square miles.
6. The ethnic composition of the population is about 80% Iranian, 16% Turkic (Azerbaijanis, etc.), and 4% Arabs and others.
7. Educational evolution is the 12th point in the "White Revolution." In 1968-1969 there were 8 universities with an enrollment of about 36,000 students, 3,000 teachers, graduating some 4,500 students. The universities include: Tehran University; National University, Tehran; Pahlavi University, Shiraz; Tabriz University; Meshed University; Isfahan University; Aryamehr University, Tehran; and Jondi Shahpur University, Ahwaz. For details about the educational system and statistics see: *Iran Almanac 1969,* pp. 493-514.

8. See the "White Revolution" for details. The six points of the document are: 1) Land reform, 3) nationalization of forests, 4) a profit sharing scheme for factory workers, 5) amendment of the electoral law, and 6) creation of a Literary Corps to strengthen education in rural areas. Other reforms were added to the above, so that there are 12 points. See *Iran Almanac 1969*, pp. 479-480.
9. For information on social welfare see: *Iran Almanac 1969*, pp. 483-484, and 485-492, 559.
10. For educational developments see: *Iran Almanac 1969*, pp. 492-513. Since 1945, there have been about 100,000 university graduates. About half of these were educated abroad, and 50% of those sent abroad studied in the United States. By 1972, 92% of urban children and 55% of rural children will be at a primary school. There are over 100 technical schools. It is hoped to reduce the illiteracy rate which is over 60% now, to 43% by 1972.
11. See U.S. Department of Labor. Bureau of Labor Statistics. Division of Foreign Labor. *Labor Practices in Iran*. Washington, D. C., G.P.O., 1963-67, and *Iran Almanac 1969*, pp. 527-528.
12. *Iran Almanac 1969*, pp. 552-556.
13. *Ibid.*, pp. 479, 559, 483-484 (Social Insurance).
14. The following books were found useful: Ann K. Lambton, *Landlord and Peasant in Persia*. Oxford, 1953; Doreen Warriner, *Land Reform and Development in the Middle East*. Oxford, 1962; J. P. Hittinger, *Planning for Agricultural Development: The Iranian Experience*. Washington, D. C., National Planning Association, 1965; Paul W. English, *City and Village in Iran*. Madison: University of Wisconsin, 1966; Norman Jacobs, *The Sociology of Development: Iran Case Study*. New York: Praeger, 1966; Reza A. Arasteh, *Man and Society in Iran*. Leiden: Brill, 1964; Amir Birjandi, *The Education Corps Prospect in Iran: A Work Plan for Development*. Tehran: Ministry of Education, 1965; Jahangir Amuzegar, *Technical Assistance in Theory and Practice: The Case of Iran*. New York: Praeger, 1966; G. H. Kazemian, *Impact of U.S. Technical Aid on the Rural Development of Iran*. New York, Gaus, 1968; *Fourth National Development Plan (1968-1972)* Tehran: Plan Organization, 1968; and Hassan Arsenjani, *Implementation of Iran's Land Reform Program*. Tehran: Keyhan Press, 1962. Also useful sources for factual information are: *Keyhan Year Book*, Tehran, 1969, and *Salnameye Keshvare Iran*. Tehran, 1969.

CHAPTER VII

Problems of Economic Development

IRAN IS PREDOMINANTLY an agricultural country, with some 60% of the people living in rural areas. However, Iran relies heavily on oil revenues to provide government income and foreign exchange. With the nationalization of the oil industry in 1951, these revenues were cut off temporarily. Oil revenues were restored in 1954 after a settlement was concluded with a consortium of international companies of which the United States holds 40%, Britain 40%, the Netherlands 14%, and France 6%. Iran signed oil concession agreements with the Standard Oil Company of Indiana in 1958, and also with the Italian National Oil Company. During 1965 six more joint-venture agreements were signed by the National Iranian Oil Company and international oil companies for oil exploration and production in the Persian Gulf. A profit-sharing contract agreement for exploration and production in offshore and inland concession areas was signed with a French Government company in 1966.[1]

Iran's oil revenues have risen from $89.6 million in 1955 to over $900 million in 1970. The Government has devoted an increasing percentage of oil revenues to economic development. In 1955 60% of the oil revenue was channeled to development, whereas the percentage went up to 80% in 1968. Until 1967, economic development also used U.S. Agency for International Development (A.I.D.) funds, but the American aid program was phased out as Iran's economy was stabilized. Loans from the Export-Import Bank, the International Bank for Reconstruction and Development (I.B.R.D.), and other international financial institutions have been available. General objectives of the various development plans have been economic growth, increased employment, and better distribution of income through implementation of social and economic reforms.

The first comprehensive and systematic effort at development was initiated in 1955 with the Second Development Plan.[2] Expenditures, however, soon outstripped sources of revenue. By 1960 Iran was faced with balance-of-payments problems and some inflation. A stabilization program was launched late in 1960 with the help of the International Monetary Fund (I.M.F.). This resulted in a minor recession which lasted to 1964. However, after 1964 a business upswing started which is still going strong.[3] During the Third Development Plan (1962-1968) the economy made remarkable progress.[4] Under the Third Plan existing industries were expanded, work was begun on iron and steel, petrochemical, and aluminum industries, and infrastructure projects were expanded.

The Fourth Development Plan (1968-1973) projects a 9% annual increase in national income, and provides a total investment of $10.9 billion in economic development projects. This should raise per capita income to $405 by 1973 (GNP per capita was $304 in 1969), allowing for normal population growth. Of the total investment, $6.8 billion is expected to come from the Iranian Government, the balance from private sources. The Plan stresses an increase in industrial, mineral, and agricultural production, with special emphasis on the completion of the iron and steel, petrochemical, aluminum projects begun under the previous plan. Water resources will also be developed in Khuzistan and the Ghazvin plain. The plan allocated $866 million to agriculture and cattle breeding, and contemplates doubling the country's present electrical generating capacity. A microwave telecommunication network is also planned. About 80% of Iran's oil revenues are to be allocated to the Plan Organization during the Fourth Plan period. The Plan emphasizes industrial development, transportation, and agriture, calls for public and private sector expenditures. So far, the Plan appears to be working well and is on schedule.[5]

Iran's exports in 1968 totalled $1.96 billion, 81% of which were petroleum products. Other exports were carpets and agricultural products, including cotton and fruits. Major export markets were (excluding petroleum) U.S.S.R. (16%); West Germany (15%); United States (11%); and Japan.

Imports valued at over $1.20 billion came largely from West Germany (23%); the United States (18%;) the United Kingdom (12%); and Japan. Major imports include machinery, iron and steel, chemicals, drugs, and electrical equipment.[6]

Excluding exports of oil, Iran traditionally has had an unfavorable balance of trade. However, Iran's balance of payments position is good because of oil revenues. In order to promote its exports and acquire imports without the expenditure of foreign exchange, Iran has entered into a number of bilateral trade and payments agreements with the U.S.S.R. and Eastern European countries. A trade agreement with the European Economic Community (EEC) has been concluded which gives tariff preference and a quota for Iranian exports of carpets, dried fruits, and caviar to the EEC. No tariff preferences are given by Iran to EEC exports. In 1964, Iran, Turkey, and Pakistan established the Regional Cooperation for Development (RCD) organization which is trying to integrate economic development, lowering tariffs, and establishing joint air and shipping lines.

Iran has a reasonably liberal trade policy. Trade is conducted generally on a multi-lateral, nondiscriminatory basis, while exports are subject to government control. Foreign exchange is available for authorized imports. Nonauthorized imports include locally produced and consumer items. Tariffs and commercial profit taxes are levied on most imports.

Total national budgeted expenditures for the year ending March 21, 1970 amounted to $5.4 billion, up from $4.4 billion budgeted in the previous year.

Total U.S. economic loans and grants through June 30, 1967 amounted to $943.1 million. The U.S. aid program was terminated November 30, 1967.

The Iranian economy is sound. Agricultural crops include wheat, rice, barley, fresh and dried fruits and vegetables. Mining is limited, except for petroleum, which is the country's most important natural resources. Other resources include iron, chrome, copper, lead, and zinc ores. There is also coal, gypsum, limestone, barite, and salt. In 1968, 1,039 million barrels of crude oil was produced. Apart from petroleum, industrial development is at an early stage. Iron and steel, petrochemicals, and aluminum plants are under development. The major industries include textiles, food processing, building materials, and rubber tires.

Iran is an ideal country for private investment because of the following reasons: political stability, abundance of natural resources, adaptable labor at reasonable cost, availability of local bank credit, expanding consumer market, rising standard of living, favorable taxes for newly-established enterprises, duty-free import capital goods for approved industries, repatriation of capital and profits up to 100%.

Investment opportunities exist in many fields including: foundries, fertilizers and pesticides, agriculture and animal husbandry, tanning and leather goods, food processing and packaging, wines and spirits, timber and wood products, ready-made clothing and footwear, chemical products, mining, porcelain and glassware.

U.S. direct private investment is estimated at $300 million, the bulk in petroleum. Government policy designed to attract investment has resulted in increased foreign investment. The Law for the Attraction and Protection of Foreign Investment was passed in 1955.

The monetary and banking policy in Iran is determined by the Currency and Credit Council established in 1960. The Government-owned Central Bank of Iran (*Bank Markazi*) established in 1960 and capitalized at 3.6 billion rials, performs the usual functions of a central bank, including currency issue and control of foreign exchange.

The Government-owned Bank Melli, which was established in 1927, and capitalized at 2 billion rials, is the largest commercial bank. Other important commercial banks include Bank Sepah, the Export Bank of Iran and the Middle East. Other banks are the Agriculture Credit and Rural Development Bank, which makes loans to farmers, and the Industrial and Mining Development Bank, which makes medium and long term loans and investments in the industrial sector. In 1968 there were 26 banks operating in Iran.[7]

The long range economic outlook for Iran is favorable. Iran's economy has achieved a high rate of growth during the last five years, aided by rising revenues paid to the Government by foreign oil companies operating in Iran.[8]

In spite of the high growth rate there has been little inflation because the government regulates prices of major consumer products, and because of increased agricultural production. The Development Plan will generate requirements for capital goods and equipment, but as the country's industrialization reaches maturity, the balance of trade may improve.

The main problems of economic development have been the lack of trained technical personnel, the need for foreign exchange to import capital goods, and new problems generated in a country in transition from a developing country to one that will become self-sufficient in most essential products. While great progress was achieved during the last decade in the economic life of the country, the prospects for the next decade appear to be even brighter.

NOTES ON CHAPTER VII

1. During the Spring of 1970 an agreement was concluded between Iran and Pakistan to use Iranian crude oil in future refinery development.

2. The First Seven Year Plan went into operation in 1949, but nationalization of the oil industry in 1951 caused a financial crisis which brought the Plan to a halt. During the Second Seven Year Plan (September 1955-September 1962), investment amounted to $4 billion, divided equally between the public and private sector. The Plan Organization, the agency responsible for public investment, had expenditures of $1.15 billion for the seven year period. By 1962, 55% of Iran's oil revenues were being used to finance Plan Organization investments. The Plan involved the building of dams, agriculture, industry, transportation, communications, and educational development.

3. The Third Development Plan (September 1962-March 1968), 5½ years, called for a total public outlay of $2.67 billion. The Plan's objectives included raising the GNP by 6% annually, creating new jobs, increasing consumer goods output, and achieving a more equitable distribution of income. The Plan had to be revised in order to take into consideration the land reform program after 1963.

4. After 1965 Iran's economy began an upsurge which increased the GNP considerably. Iran's GNP was estimated at $8.3 billion in 1969, up 10% from 1968. Per capita GNP was $304 in 1969. In 1970 GNP reached $9.0 billion, per capita GNP is now $321. The following were found useful on recent economy of Iran: "Iran's Economic Upsurge," *Middle East Journal,* Autumn, 1967; George B. Baldwin, *Planning and Development in Iran.* Baltimore, 1967; *Iran: A Trade and Industrial Profile.* New York: Manhattan Publishing Co., 1969; *Basic Data on the Economy of Iran.* Department of Commerce, OBR 68-64, Washington, D. C., July 1968; E.I.U. Quarterly Economic Reviews. *IRAN: Annual Supplement 1969.* London: The Economist Intelligence Unit, 1969; *Iran: Background Notes.* Department of State. Washington, D. C., publication 7760, February, 1970.

5. See *Iran Almanac 1969,* pp. 246-470 for information on the economy of Iran. Development plans are discussed on pages 389-394.

6. *Ibid.,* pp. 273-388 (foreign trade data). More recent trade figures arrived before publication and are shown below:

Exports.—1969 exports valued at $2,024 million, including $1,807 million in petroleum (1968, $1,961 million, including $1,780 in petroleum). Major export markets (including petroleum): Japan (32%); United Kingdom (18%); India (6%); United States (4%). Major non-oil exports: carpets, cotton, fruits, hides, and leather products.

Imports.—1969 imports valued at $1,423 million (1968, $1,206 million). Major suppliers: W. Germany (21%); United States (17%); United Kingdom (13%). Major imports: Machinery, iron and steel, medicines and chemicals, electrical equipment.

7. Iranian currency: U.S. $1.00 = 75 rials; 1 rial = 100 dinars; 10 rials = 1 toman.
8. Charles Issawi, and Mohammed Yeganeh, *The Economics of Middle Eastern Oil.* New York: Praeger, 1963; George Lenczowski, *Oil and State in the Middle East,* Ithaca, 1960; see also *Iran Almanac 1969,* Petroleum, pp. 321-345, Iran is the fourth largest petroleum producing country in the world.

CHAPTER VIII

Iran in World Affairs

DURING THE 19TH CENTURY Iran was faced with threats to its independence and territorial integrity by Tsarist Russia. The Treaty of Gulistan (1813), and the Treaty of Turk-manchai (1828) were imposed on Iran by Russia. The British too were involved in Iran and rivaled the Russians. Iran was also the victim of European imperialism under the capitulations.[1]

Iran's cultural and social contacts with the West, including the British and the American missionaries, educators, and doctors is traced to the 1830's.[2] Formal diplomatic relations with the United States started in 1883. At the dawn of the 20th century, Iran was caught in the struggle between Russia and Britain in the Middle East. Iran sought the help of a third disinterested power against the Anglo-Russian threat. "The natural choice was the United States."[3] The American policy of non-involvement during this period, expressed by the Monroe Doctrine prevented direct United States support.[4] However, the United States did respond to the Iranian request for financial advisors in 1911. The American advisors were private citizens and not U.S. officials. The Shuster Mission strengthened Iranian-American friendship. Unfortunately, Anglo-Russian pressures forced Mr. Shuster to leave Iran.[5]

Two other American missions were faced with Anglo-Russian pressures. Dr. Arthur C. Millspaugh led a mission in 1922-1927, and another one during 1942-1945.[6] While

63

some of the recommendations and actions of these missions were helpful to Iran, the personality of Dr. Millspaugh and the sensitivity of the emerging Iranian nationalism to what they considered foreign interference created tensions. Also, the usual Anglo-Russian pressures further acerbated the situation.

Russia was a constant threat to Iran since the Treaty of Gulistan and before. After the 1917 Bolshevik Revolution, the Communists claimed that they had given up the imperialism of the Tsars. However, they hoped to win support for Communism in the Muslim World, and Iran became a target of Communist propoganda. The chaotic conditions in Iran after World War I, and the weak government of the Qajars made Iran a potentially attractive place for the designs of the Communists. In 1920 a Communist Party was organized in Iran which later became the Tudeh Party (Masses).

As a result of the new Russian policies, a Treaty of Friendship between Iran (Persia), and the Russian Socialist Federal Soviet Republic was signed in Moscow, February 26, 1921. An exchange of notes to rectify some differences took place on December 21, 1921, and the Treaty was ratified on February 26, 1922.[7] The Treaty opened with the characteristic Communist claims of friendship for workers and peasants of Iran, and denounced Tsarist and European colonialism. Among its provisions were: the frontiers and independence of each of the signatories were to be respected; Iranian debts to Russia were declared cancelled; former concessions held by Russia in Iran were to be relinquished by the Soviets, except the Caspian Sea fisheries; it was agreed that neither power would harbor the enemies of the other; and if a third power were to threaten or occupy any part of Iran, the Soviets would send troops to Iran (Article VI). Article VI was to cause problems for Iran later. Also, Article XIII, which made Iran promise not to cede to any other foreign power or national thereof, privileges or concessions relinquished by the Soviets, created problems in the future.

Soviet threats to Iran during the period 1921-1923 were resisted by Reza Khan, who later became Reza Shah Pahlavi.

During the period before the Second World War, Iran developed close relations with Germany. However, Iran finally sided with the Allies in 1941. In January 1942 a Treaty of Alliance between the United Kingdom and the Soviet Union, and Iran was signed. The Lend-Lease Act of March 1942 resulted in American aid to Iran. The Tripartite Treaty (1942) and the Tehran Declaration (1943) were milestones in the diplomatic history of Iran. It was during this time that the Schwarzkopf Mission (1943-1948) helped Iran organize its Gendarmerie. The Persian Gulf Command while useful in getting aid to the Soviets who were fighting the Axis, created problems for Iran as incidents involving American troops resulted in anti-American feeling among the Iranian people.

In 1945 a serious crisis developed which threatened the territorial integrity of northern Iran. However, the crisis ended with an Iranian victory, when the Shah's troops liberated Azerbaijan in 1946.[8]

In 1948, the Iranian Government asked the Anglo-Iranian Oil Company (AIOC) to give Iran a larger share of the company's profits. The AIOC refused to do this. Things became more urgent in 1950 when the United States failed to grant Iran a badly needed loan for the vital Seven Year Plan. Premier Razmara, urged the AIOC to make some concessions, since other countries such as Venezuela and Saudi Arabia had obtained better terms. The failure of the AIOC, to act and its interference in Iran's internal affairs, created anti-British feelings. It was felt that the United States favored the British despite the fact that Americans tried to remain neutral. The *Majlis* voted to nationalize the oil industry. Thus on March 15, 1951 this important decision was made which would have serious consequences. General Razmara was an effective Prime Minister and nationalization under his control would have been effective. However, when Dr. Mossadegh became Premier on April 30, 1951, the outlawed Tudeh Party resumed its activities. On May 1, 1951 Tudeh members demonstrated waving red flags and shouting anti-imperialist slogans. Soviet broadcasts supported the Tudeh and attacked the Iranian Government and the "imperialists." Since Mossadegh was anti-British he thought it was a good idea to cooperate with the Tudeh. This was to lead to his downfall.

The AIOC and the British Government protested the nationalization, but the Iranians stood firm. Negotiations broke down by August 1951, and a deadlock ensued which lasted until the overthrow of Dr. Mossadegh in 1953.

In September 1951, Britain ordered an embargo on Iranian oil. By 1952 Iran's economy was badly shaken. Premier Mossadegh demanded more power to cope with the deteriorating situation. In October 1952, Iran severed diplomatic relations with the British. Iranians could not understand why the oil companies and even the Americans complied with the embargo. This created some anti-American sentiment, especially as the Communist broadcasts stressed American perfidy.

By January 1953, Mossadegh's coalition began to disintegrate, and by the end of August, 1953, his failure to settle the oil dispute had alienated most of his former backers in the *Majlis*. Mossadegh tried to rule by decree, became authoritarian, and even called for the creation of a Republic. He was finally ousted on August 19, 1953 by the Shah's supporters. Although the United States had again tried to remain neutral in this dispute, Americans tried to help find a compromise solution. The National Iranian Oil Company (NIOC) was formed, and the oil dispute was finally resolved during 1954, when an agreement was signed with a consortium. The way to economic recovery was now possible.

One of the most important decisions of Iranian foreign policy took place in October 1955, when Iran aligned itself with the West by joining the Baghdad Pact (now the Central Treaty Organization, or CENTO). Iran maintained this posture despite considerable Soviet pressure. Iran's political and economic relations with Western Europe have become closer since 1962, and a number of important trade and aid agreements were signed.

After several years of strained relations marked by a persistent Soviet propaganda campaign directed against Iran, Soviet-Iranian relations took a more cordial turn in September 1962, when Iran removed Soviet fears by declaring that it would not permit foreign missiles to be based on Iranian soil. Relations with the Soviet Union and East European countries are now normal and involve some economic assistance and an increasing amount of barter trade.

Iran's relations with Israel has generally been good. Iran's current foreign affairs preoccupations largely involve relations with certain Arab states. After strained relations with the United Arab Republic, Iraq, and Lebanon, in the last few months, a return to better relations has taken place. Tension with Iraq over the Shatt-al-Arab which flared up recently has been contained. Nearby Arab countries are of increasing importance as the United Kingdom prepares to withdraw militarily from the areas of the Persian Gulf in close proximity to Iran.[9] Iran has worked to achieve good relations with Saudi Arabia, Kuwait, and the Persian Gulf Sheikhdoms now in special treaty relations with the British. The future of Bahrain[10] has been an area of disagreement with the Arabs, but recently both Iran and the Arab states have agreed to an amicable solution with the help of the United Nations. Iran has also participated in a number of Islamic conferences.

Iran's relations with Turkey and Pakistan are extremely close. The Iranian-Turkish-Pakistani cooperation continues in CENTO, as the three Middle Eastern countries work toward defense and economic integration. Iranian-American relations are also cordial. The United States helped Iran maintain its independence in the difficult days after the war.

American aid in the past helped Iran to make social and economic progress. Iran, as a member of CENTO, has developed collective defense security arrangements and has strengthened its economic and cultural ties with its regional CENTO partners. The United States has extended such assistance as sales of surplus agricultural commodities (Public Law 480) required by the Iranian supply situation, technical assistance for economic development, and military assistance. The U.S. Aid Mission was closed on November 30, 1967, as Iran's improved economic conditions no longer necessitated reliance on foreign aid. There still is a Peace Corps contingent in Iran.

Today Iran, one of the most stable and united countries in the Middle East, is using its good offices to work for the peace and prosperity of the area. The Shah has taken the initiative to seek the support of neighboring countries to work for peace and mutual cooperation. The Shah, President Sunay of Turkey, and President Yahya of Pakistan have met frequently. During May 1970, Iran, Pakistan, and Turkey met in a summit meeting in Izmir, where they discussed a series of political and economic matters.[11]

Despite their various alliances and ties with the West and the United States, Iran, Pakistan, and Turkey are developing a more independent role in foreign affairs, through an organization established in 1964 to coordinate economic projects. This organization, known as the Regional Cooperation for Development (RCD), has not yet been converted into a political pact. However, these three Middle Eastern countries are closely aligning their policies on joint and regional problems and their leaders and diplomats are in constant consultation with each other.[12]

During the Izmir summit held during May 1970, the leaders of Iran, Pakistan, and Turkey sent messages to President Nixon and Premier Kosygin urging them to use their influence to bring peace to the Middle East, and bring about Israel's withdrawal from occupied Arab territory in compliance with the U.N. Security Council's resolution of

November 1967. They also expressed opposition to Israel's changing unilaterally the status of Jerusalem.

The three countries decided to keep CENTO in being during the May, 1970, meeting. They also decided on a number of measures to increase their economic ties. In addition to reducing trade barriers, they have cooperated on a number of joint industrial projects. They agreed to integrate the operation of their airlines, and cooperated in shipping and other transportation matters. Progress was also reported in the building of a railroad connecting the three countries on new communication links. Cultural exchange has also been stressed.

One can conclude by stating that today the Shah's successful diplomacy has resulted in continued close relations with the West and the United States; it has made possible a detente with the Soviet Bloc, and has further strengthened cooperation among Middle Eastern countries through CENTO, RCD, and Islamic conferences.[13]

One can sum up the events of the last decade by saying —Iran's achievements in the domestic field have been matched by its successes in the diplomatic sphere.[14]

NOTES ON CHAPTER VIII

1. Matin Daftary, *La suppression des capitulations en Perse.* Paris, 1930.
2. D. M. Finnie, *Pioneers East.* Cambridge, 1967. (Chapter VIII).
3. Mehdi Heravi, *Iranian-American Diplomacy.* New York: Gaus, 1969,
4. For the principles of the Monroe Doctrine see: Dexter Perkins, *Hands Off: The Monroe Doctrine.* Boston, 1948.
   p. 114.
5. W. M. Shuster, *The Strangling of Persia.* New York, 1912.
6. Arthur C. Millspaugh, *The Financial and Economic Situation in Persia.* Boston, 1926, and by the same author *Americans in Persia.* Washington, D. C., 1946. See also Mehdi Heravi, *Iranian-American Diplomacy.* New York: Gaus, 1969, Chapter V.
7. For details of the 1921 Treaty see: *British and Foreign State Papers,* Vol. 114, pp. 901-909; J. C. Hurewitz, *ed., Diplomacy in the Near and Middle East: A Documentary Record.* Princeton, 1956, Vol. II, p. 90; H. M. Davis, *Constitutions* etc., Durham, N. C., 1947, pp. 90-100; and Mehdi Heravi, *ed., Encyclopedia of the Middle East.* Washington, D. C., Public Affairs Press, 1971.

8. William Eagleton, Jr. *The Kurdish Republic of 1946.* Oxford, 1963; George Lenczowski, *Russia and the West in Iran, 1918-1948.* Ithaca: Cornell, 1949.

9. William D. Brewer, "Yesterday and Tomorrow in the Persian Gulf," *Middle East Journal,* Spring 1969. See also: Center for Strategic and International Studies. *The Gulf: Implications of British Withdrawal.* Washington, D. C., Special Report Series No. 8, February 1969.

10. Fereydoun Adamiyat, *Bahrein Islands: Legal and Diplomatic Study of the British Iranian Controversy.* New York: Praeger, 1955.

11. This was the fourth such meeting. The first was held in Istanbul in 1964, when the RCD was established. The second summit was held at Ramsar, Iran, in 1967. The third meeting was held in Karachi, Pakistan, in 1968. The next summit is scheduled for next year in Iran.

12. Turkey is a member of NATO, Pakistan of SEATO, and all three belong to CENTO, with which Britain and the United States are also associated.

13. See also: Firuz Kazemzadeh, *Russia and Britain in Persia, 1864-1914.* Yale, 1968; Rouhallah K. Ramazani, *The Foreign Policy of Iran, 1500-1941.* University of Virginia, 1966; Rouhallah K. Ramazani, *The Northern Tier.* Princeton: Van Nostrand, 1966; N. S. Fatemi, *Diplomatic History of Persia.* New York, 1952; Peter W. Avery, *Modern Iran.* London, 1965; John Marlow, *Iran: A Short Political Guide.* New York, 1963; and Donald N. Wilber, *Contemporary Iran.* New York, 1963.

14. The Iranian Army is a defensive force of 200,000. There are also naval and air forces. Iran is a member of CENTO, and has received considerable military aid from the United States. See *Iran Almanac 1969* for details. Armed Forces pp. 131-136, Gendarmerie and Police, pp. 137-139.

CHAPTER IX

Conclusions

IRAN IS A COUNTRY with an illustrious past. The greatness of Iran was in Ancient and Medieval times, when Iranian culture and civilization flourished.

As in the case of the Turkish Empire, Iranian greatness declined after the 16th century. During the course of the 19th century, Iran found itself caught between the Russian expansionism from the north and the British in India to the south. The intense Anglo-Russian rivalry was temporarily resolved by the 1907 Anglo-Russian Convention, when the rise of Germany added a new dimension to European imperialism in the strategically significant area of the Middle East.

Despite the stirrings of Iranian nationalism against foreign interference in Iranian affairs, and an effort at constitutional reform, the Qajar dynasty was unable to cope with the external and internal threats to Iran's national sovereignty. Although anxious to remain neutral in the First World War, Iran was overrun by the belligerent powers. Conditions went from bad to worse in the post-war period, but a great leader arose to save the nation in the tradition of Shah Abbas, Nadir Shah, and Shah Ismail Safavi. A new dynasty was established in 1925, and Reza Shah Pahlavi the Great laid down the foundations of modern Iran during his reign which lasted from 1925 to 1941. He was succeeded by his eldest son, Mohammad Reza Shah, who continued his father's modernization reforms and guided Iran safely through the war years.

During the Second World War, Iran sided with the Allied Powers. The "Persian Corridor" was of special importance to the Allies as a route to supply the hard-pressed Russians. Iranian cooperation and the achievements of the Persian Gulf Command contributed significantly to the final victory.

Iran had joined the United Nations and had contributed to the general struggle against the Axis Powers. After the war, the British and Americans withdrew their forces from Iran in conformity with the 1942 Tripartite Treaty of Alliance. However, it took a serious confrontation to force Soviet troop withdrawals during 1945-1946. The courageous leadership of the Shah, and United States and United Nations support finally led to the liberation of Azerbaijan in 1946.

During the post-war period Mohammad Reza Shah strengthened Iran's external and internal position. However, in the early 1950's, continued Soviet threats and blandishments led to an internal crisis which threatened to destroy the nation. At this time, the nationalization of the oil industry created financial problems which further acerbated the situation. But again, the effective leadership of the Shah, the loyalty of the overwhelming majority of the people, and the support of the Armed Forces saved the day.

Following the 1951-1953 internal crisis which had affected the economy of the country adversely, the ill effects of the nationalization of the oil industry were overcome by 1954, and oil revenues which had been halted began to provide increased resources for the social and economic uplift of the country.

In 1955 Iran sought mutual security in the Baghdad Pact (later known as CENTO). Changing circumstances and new developments in the world have resulted in shifts in Iranian foreign policy. While Iran remains a staunch friend of the United States and the West, the Iranian leadership has through astute diplomacy achieved a detente in relations with the Soviet Bloc, resulting in increased trade.

The Shah's diplomatic successes were duplicated in the domestic field. A program of reforms started in the mid-1950's reached a climax in 1963, when the Shah introduced his reform program, later to be known as the "White Revolution." The "White Revolution" aimed at the modernization of the whole of Iranian society, thus stealing the thunder from the Communists and extreme-leftist elements.

This Revolution has become the basis of the new reform program and is summarized here because of its importance to the whole nation.

During the course of a Congress of Iranian Farm Cooperatives, the Shah suggested a series of far-reaching reforms. These reforms were presented to the people, and a referendum was held on January 26, 1963, and the six points of reform, given below, were overwhelmingly approved by the people.

1. The abolition of the landlord-serf situation through the approval of the land reforms in Iran on the basis of the Land Reforms (Amendment) Law dated January 9, 1962, and further amendments thereto.

2. Approval of the Decree-Law for the nationalization of forests throughout the country.

3. Approval of the Decree-Law for the sale of Government-owned factories to be used as backing for land reforms.

4. Amendment of the Election Law.

5. Approval of the Decree-Law for workers' profit sharing scheme.

6. Decree-Law for the creation of the Literacy Corps aimed at facilitating the implementation of the university and compulsory education law.

When the above six reforms were carried out, three more were added:

7. Creation of the Health Corps.

8. Creation of the Extension and Development Corps.
9. Creation of the Houses of Justice.

These reforms were also effected swiftly, allowing for the adoption of three more measures, announced by His Imperial Majesty during the opening of the new term of the *Majlis* on October 6, 1967:

10. Nationalization of the water resources of the country.
11. Reconstruction of the country.
12. Administrative and educational revolution.

The Shahanshah Arya Mehr in the meeting of the Economic Council held on September 20, 1965, observed that:

> We believe that Iran should follow a policy which is essential to it. We know better which policy is better for Iran. It is quite likely that in one respect this policy may coincide with the principles of capitalism and in other respects either with socialism or even communism. The Government's attitude does not depend on the nomenclature or on the policy of that nomenclature, but on the work or services for the good of the people.[1]

Thus, the Iranian leadership adapted a pragmatic approach to solve the problems of the country instead of trying to resist change or become the victim of permissive policies leading to chaos.

It is fitting to end our story with the Coronation in 1967, which heralded the birth of a new era. The celebration of the 2500th Anniversary of the Founding of the Iranian Monarchy, was announced during August 1968.[2] These celebrations of the heritage of the past are important to the Iranian people because they hold the promise of the future.

NOTES ON CHAPTER IX

1. *Iran Almanac 1969*, pp. 479-480.
2. Cyrus the Great (559 B.C.-530 B.C.) is considered the first Iranian (Persian) monarch. A Council of Celebrations and a number of committees have been formed. These celebrations have received wide publicity not only in Iran but in the whole world. For details see *Iran Almanac 1969*, pp. 50-54.

Selected Bibliography

AMERICAN UNIVERSITY. Foreign Area Studies Division. *Area Handbook for Iran*. Washington: Government Printing Office, 1963.

AMUZEGAR, JAHANGIR. *Technical Assistance in Theory and Practice: The Case of Iran*. New York: Frederick A. Praeger, 1966.

ARBERRY, A. J., ed. *The Legacy of Persia*. New York: Oxford University Press, 1953.

ARFA, HASSAN. *Under Five Shahs*. New York: William Morrow and Co., 1965.

AVERY, PETER. *Modern Iran*. New York: Frederick A. Praeger, 1965.

BALDWIN, GEORGE B. *Planning and Development in Iran*. Baltimore: The Johns Hopkins Press, 1967.

BANANI, AMIN. *The Modernization of Iran, 1921-1941*. Palo Alto: Stanford University Press, 1962.

BENEDICK, RICHARD E. *Industrial Finance in Iran*. Cambridge: Harvard University Graduate School of Business Administration, 1964.

BINDER, LEONARD. *Iran: Political Development in a Changing Society*. Berkeley: University of California Press, 1962.

CHURCHILL, ROGERS P. *The Anglo-Persian Convention*. Iowa, Cedar Rapids: The Torch Press, 1939.

COTTAM, RICHARD W. *Nationalism in Iran*. Pittsburgh: University of Pittsburgh Press, 1964.

CULICAN, WILLIAM. *The Medes and the Persians*. New York: Frederick A. Praeger, 1965.

ENGLISH, PAUL WARD. *City and Village in Iran: Settlement and Economy in the Kirman Basin*. Madison: University of Wisconsin Press, 1966.

FERDOWSI. *The Epic of the Kings: Shah-Nama the National Epic of Persia*. Chicago: University of Chicago Press, 1966.

FRYE, RICHARD N. *The Heritage of Persia*. New York: Mentor Books, 1966.

————. *Iran*. New York: Holt, Rinehart and Winston, 1953.

HANDLEY-TAYLOR, G. *Bibliography of Iran*. New York: International Publication Service, 1968.

HERAVI, MEHDI. *Iranian-American Diplomacy*. New York: T. Gaus Sons, 1969.

HITTINGER, J. PRICE. *Planning for Agricultural Development: The Iranian Experience.* Washington: National Planning Association, 1965.

JACOBS, NORMAN. *The Sociology of Development: Iran as an Asian Case Study.* New York: Frederick A. Praeger, 1966.

KAZEMIAN, GHOLAM H. *Impact of U.S. Technical Aid on the Rural Development of Iran.* New York: T. Gaus Sons, 1968.

KAZEMZADEH, FIRUZ. *Russia and Britain in Persia, 1864-1914.* New Haven: Yale University Press, 1968.

KEDDIE, NIKKI R. *Religion and Rebellion in Iran.* London: Frank Cass and Co., 1966.

LAMBTON, A. K. S. *Landlord and Peasant in Persia.* New York: Oxford University Press, 1953.

LENCZOWSKI, GEORGE. *Russia and the West in Iran, 1918-1948: A Study in Big Power Rivalry.* Ithaca: Cornell University Press, 1949.

MARLOWE, JOHN. *Iran: A Short Political Guide.* New York: Frederick A. Praeger, 1963.

MEHDEVI, ANNE. *Persia Revisited.* New York: Alfred A. Knopf, 1964.

PAHLAVI, H.I.M. MOHAMMAD REZA SHAH, Shahanshah of Iran. *Mission for My Country.* New York: McGraw-Hill Book Co., 1961.

RAMAZANI, ROUHALLAH. *The Foreign Policy of Iran, 1500-1941.* Charlottesville: University Press of Virginia, 1966.

SARAN, P., *ed., Persian Documents.* New York: Asia Publishing House, 1968.

SYKES, SIR PERCY. *A History of Persia.* New York: St. Martin's Press, 1930.

UPTON, JOSEPH M. *The History of Modern Iran: An Interpretation.* Cambridge: Harvard University Press, 1960.

WILBER, DONALD N. *Contemporary Iran.* New York: Frederick A. Praeger, 1963.

————. *Iran: Past and Present.* Princeton: Princeton University Press, 1962.

APPENDIX A

H.I.M. the Shahanshah Arya Mehr's Address on the Occasion of the New Year[1]

I CONGRATULATE the Iranian nation on the occasion of Nowruz and wish you all happiness, health, and ever-increasing prosperity.

The past year was a fruitful and successful year for our people. We managed to achieve a 9.5% growth rate at constant prices during this period. This is higher than the figure envisaged for the Fourth Plan. Our GNP growth rate for the period was nearly 13% at current prices. However, owing to circumstances beyond our control, particularly higher international commodity prices, including high prices of steel and other goods which had to be imported from abroad, prices were 3.5% higher this year than the previous year. It should be borne in mind that international interest rates remained higher during this period. This naturally had some effect on our domestic prices.

In addition to investments in existing industries, 90 new plants with a total investment of 13.5 billion rials started operations in the past year. The most important were two great petrochemical plants at Abadan and Kharg, a steel rolling plant, a nylon fibre plant, a sugar refining mill, a plant for producing transformers, and a cement factory. During the same period, power generating industry—a lever in the country's social and industrial expansion drive—expanded considerable. On the Pub-

---

[1] Excerpts from the Shah's Nowruz Address (March 21, 1970).

lic sector alone it achieved a 3.5% growth rate. As a result, total production amounted to 5.5 billion kilowatt-hours, making per capita consumption more than 200 kilowatt-hours.

Regarding increasing water resources, the projects initiated during the Third Plan gradually reached utilization stage. During the past year, five new storage dams with a total storage capacity of 3.8 billion cubic meters harnessed more than 5 billion cubic meters of water which used to go to waste, placing it at the disposal of Iran's economy. As a result, Iran now has 11 dams, with a total storage capacity of 9 billion cubic meters, capable of harnessing 15 billion cubic meters of water.

Many steps have been taken with regard to an administrative revolution. Although the progress achieved falls short of our expectations, it should be borne in mind, of course, that the proper achievement of such a revolution depends as much on the attitude of the employee sitting behind a desk as on the attitude of those dealing with him. Without their close cooperation in removing shortcomings, the reform will not be achieved in the desired way.

Unfortunately, spring floods in the past year caused a great deal of damage in Azerbaijan. From the agricultural standpoint, the situation has so far been very promising, and we hope, God willing, that the weather conditions will be clement enough this spring to enable a bumper harvest this year. We must, of course, aim at complete transformation of Iranian agriculture in line with latest techniques employed in the world today.

On the other hand, our factories must operate at full capacity to achieve maximum utilization at minimum cost, resulting in increased income for both the worker and employer, as well as in cheaper goods for the consumer. To achieve this, we require on the one hand, perfect management know-how, and on the other, ever-greater skills and technical ability of workers.

As I stated at the beginning of last year, the nearly doubled increase in the cost of gas pipeline and the increase in construction costs of Shahpur Petrochemical industry by 40%, could have caused some difficulties for our national economy. The difficulties were overcome by imposing certain import restrictions, and we were thus able to end the year successfully from this standpoint.

As you know, we terminated the colonial treaty on the

Arvand Rud (Shatt al-Arab) in the past year, because we believe that now that colonialism has ended in the world, it naturally cannot leave its heritage behind. However, we have always been ready to settle our differences with others peacefully on the basis of prevailing international laws.

On military matters, bearing in mind the present world situation, and in particular as long as there exists a risk to Iran's supreme interests, we cannot neglect for one moment the task of strengthening our Armed Forces for the protection of Iran's legitimate and undeniable rights so long as genuine universal disarmament has not been achieved.

The countries which have taken steps toward fundamental changes have had to ask their nations for sacrifices for one or even two generations. These nations have been called upon to eat and wear less so that their produce can be used as much as possible to strengthen the defense and economic potentials of the country. God willing, however, we have achieved for you, instead of such deprivations, a 10% annual growth rate. It is indeed a miracle, while the most far-reaching social revolution is taking place in our country, and the firmest foundations of political, economic, and military infrastructure are being laid, that the general living condition has improved so much, and economic growth and personal income have increased to such an extent. There has been no need for us to call on the Iranian people to undergo sacrifices and deprivations. I am confident, however, that were such sacrifices necessary, the Iranian nation, like any other dynamic nation, would be prepared for the task.

APPENDIX B

Chronology of Historical Events

ACHAEMENID DYNASTY

B.C.

546 Cyrus I proclaims himself King of Persia. Defeat of Croesus and capture of Sardis.
539 Capture of Babylonia.
529 Death of Cyrus I. Accession of Cambyses.
528 Conquest of Egypt.
521 Death of Cambyses. Accession of Darius I.
486 Death of Darius I. Accession of Xerxes I.
466 Accession of Artaxerxes I.
424 Accession of Xerxes II. Accession of Darius II.
404 Accession of Artaxerxes II.
358 Accession of Artaxerxes III.
336 Accession of Darius III.
330 Assassination of Darius III. Alexander captures Ecbatana. End of Achaemenids.

SELEUCIDS

320 Rise of Seleucus I Nicator.
281 Accession of Antiochus I Soter.
262 Accession of Antiochus II Theos.

PARTHIAN PERIOD

250 Arsaces I founds Parthian dynasty.
247 Accession of Arsaces II.

223 Accession of Antiochus III.
214 Accession of Arsaces III.
188 Peace of Apamea. Accession of Seleucus IV Philopator.
175 Accession of Antiochus IV.
170 Accession of Mithradates I.
162 Accession of Demetrius Soter. Decline of Seleucids.
138 Accession of Phraates II.
124 Accession of Mithradates II.
 69 Accession of Phraates III.
 60 Accession of Mithradates III.
 37 Accession of Phraates IV.
 36 Mark Anthony's Parthian expedition.
  2 Murder of Phraates IV.

A.D.

105 Accession of Osroes.
115 Trajan occupies Mesopotamia.
122 Peace between Parthia and Rome.
148 Accession of Volagasses III.
217 Death of Caracalla. Peace between Parthia and Rome.
220 Revolt of Artaxerxes (Ardashir).
226 Rout and death of Aratabanus. End of Parthian period.

SASSANIAN DYNASTY

226 Ardashir I proclaims himself Emperor of Persia.
232 Ardashir concludes peace with Rome. Annexation of Armenia.
241 Accession of Shahpur I.
260 Capture of Emperor Valerian.
272 Accession of Hormuz I.
273 Accession of Bahram I. Execution of Mani.
276 Accession of Bahram II.
293 Accession of Bahram III. Accession of Narses.
302 Accession of Hormuz II.
309 Accession of Shahpur II.
376 Peace between Rome and Persia.
379 Death of Shahpur II. Accession of Ardashir II.
383 Accession of Shahpur III.
388 Accession of Bahram IV.

399   Accession of Yazdagird I.
410   Council of Seleucia. Alaric captures Rome.
420   Accession of Bahram V (Bahram Gur).
421   Peace concluded with Rome.
438   Accession of Yazdagird II.
457   Accession of Homruz III.
459   Accession of Firuz.
483   Defeat of Firuz by White Huns. Accession of Volagases.
488   Accession of Kavadh. Campaign against Khazars. Rise of Mazdak. Kavadh deposed by Jamasp.
501   Restoration of Kavadh.
524   War with Byzantium.
529   Justinian closes Athens schools. Greek scholars flee to Persia.
531   Accession of Khosro I Anushirvan. Execution of Mazdak.
533   Peace with Byzantium.
570   Conquest of Yemen. Birth of Mohammad.
578   Death of Anushirvan. Accession of Hormuz IV.
590   Accession of Khosro II (Parviz).
591   Defeat and death of Bahram Chubin.
603   War between Byzantium and Persia.
614   Parviz captures Damascus and Jerusalem.
617   Parviz captures Chalcedon.
628   Deposition and death of Parviz. Accession of Kavadh II.
632   Accession of Yazdagird III. Death of Mohammad.
636   Persians defeated at Qadisiya.
642   Persians defeated at Nahavand. Arab domination.
651   Death of Yazdagird III.

ARAB DOMINATION

747   Abbasid rising in Khorassan under Abu Muslim.
750   End of the Omayyads. Establishment of the Abbasid Caliphate.
786   Harun al-Rashid becomes Caliph.
813   al-Ma'mun becomes Caliph.

MINOR PERSIAN DYNASTIES

820   Tahir founds the Tahirid dynasty.
872   Tahirids overthrown by Yaqub b. Laith, founder of the Saffarid dynasty.

878 Accession of Amr b. Laith.
903 Ismail b. Ahmad captures Khorassan from Saffarids. Rise of Samanid dynasty.
913 Accession of Nasr II b. Ahmad.
976 Accession of Qabus the Ziyarid.
999 Mahmud of Ghazna establishes the Ghaznavid dynasty.
1037 Rise of Seljuqs under Tughril.
1055 Tughril ends Buwayhid rule.
1072 Accession of Malik Shah.
1092 Assassination of Nizam al-Mulk.
1117 Accession of Sanjar.
1157 End of Seljuq rule in Persia. Rise of Khwarizm Shahs.
1172 Accession of Tukush.
1199 Accession of Ala' al-Din Mohammad.
1220 Accession of Jalal al-Din Mangbarti. First appearance of Mongols in Persia.
1227 Death of Genghis Khan.
1231 Overthrow of the Khwarizm Shahs.

ILKHANID AND TIMURID PERIOD

1256 Hulagu Khan appointed Ilkhan of Persia.
1258 Mongols sack Baghdad. End of Abbasid Caliphate.
1284 Accession of Arghun.
1287 Salgharid dynasty extinguished.
1295 Accession of Ghazan Mahmud.
1313 Establishment of Muzaffarid dynasty of Fars under Mubariz al-Din.
1316 Accession of Abu Said the Ilkan.
1336 Establishment of the Jalairid dynasty under Shaikh Hasan Buzurg.
1337 Establishment of the Sarbadarid dynasty in Khorassan.
1356 Accession of Shaikh Uwais the Jalairid.
1357 Accession of Shah Shuja the Muzaffarid.
1382 Accession of Sultan Asmad the Jalairid. Timur extinguishes the Sarbadars.
1393 Timur extinguishes the Muzaffarids and expels the Jalairids from Baghdad.
1405 Accession of Shah Rukh.
1447 Accession of Ulugh Beg.
1452 Accession of Abu Said the Timurid.

1466   Accession of Uzun Hasan the Aq-Quyunli of Azerbaijan.
1500   Overthrow of the Timurids.

SAFAVIDS

1502   Ismail I founds the Safavid dynasty.
1514   Battle of Chaldiran. Ismail defeated by Selim I.
1524   Accession of Tahmasp I.
1544   Humayun the Mughal Emperor a refugee in Persia.
1576   Accession of Ismail II.
1578   Accession of Mohammad Khudabanda.
1587   Accession of Abbas I the Great.
1618   Peace between Persia and Ottoman Empire.
1622   Portuguese expelled from Hormuz.
1629   Accession of Safi I.
1642   Accession of Abbas II.
1667   Accession of Sulaiman I.
1694   Accession of Husain.
1722   Afghans under Mahmud seize Isfahan. Peter the Great occupies Derbent. Accession of Tahmasp II.
1723   Russians occupy Rasht. and Baku.
1725   Accession of Ashraf the Afghan.
1729   Afghans defeated. Isfahan reoccupied.
1732   Nadir Quli dethrones Tahmasp II. Treaty of Rasht. Accession of Abbas III.
1735   Nadir Quli recovers Baku and Derbent.
1736   End of the Safavids.

AFSHARIDS

1736   Nadir Quli proclaims himself Shah of Persia.
1738   Nadir Shah's Indian conquest.
1740   Nadir Shah conquers Bukhara and Khiva.
1747   Assassination of Nadir Shah. Accession of Adil.
1748   Accession of Shah Rukh the Afsharid.

ZANDS

1750   Karim Khan occupies Southern Persia.
1779   Accession of Ali Murad.
1785   Accession of Jafar.

1789 Accession of Luft Ali.
1794 Aqa Mohammed Qajar overthrows Luft Ali. End of the Zand dynasty.

QAJARS

1795 Aqa Mohammad invades Georgia. Capture of Tiflis and Erivan.
1796 Coronation of Aqa Mohammad.
1797 Assassination of Aqa Mohammed. Accession of Fath Ali Shah.
1813 Treaty of Gulistan. Persia cedes extensive territories to Russia.
1827 Russia seizes Tabriz.
1828 Treaty of Turkmanchai.
1834 Accession of Mohammad Shah.
1848 Accession of Nasir al-Din.
1865 Russians capture Tashkent.
1868 Russians occupy Samarkand.
1873 Russians conquer Khiva.
1876 Russians annex Khokand.
1896 Assassination of Nasir al-Din. Accession of Muzaffar al-Din Shah.
1906 Promulgation of the Persian Constitution. Death of Muzaffar al-Din Shah.
1907 Accession of Mohammad Ali Shah. Overthrow of Constitution. Anglo-Russian Convention.
1908 Nationalist uprising.
1909 Abdication of Mohammad Ali Shah. Accession of Ahmad Shah.
1911 Shuster Mission.
1921 Russo-Persian Treaty. Reza Khan becomes Commander-in-Chief of Army and Minister of War.
1922 Millspaugh Mission (1922-1927).
1923 Reza Shah becomes Prime Minister. Shah Ahmad leaves for Europe.

PAHLAVIS

1925 Special Constituent Assembly proclaims Reza Khan Shahinshah of Iran. Pahlavi dynasty founded.

1941 The Allied forces invade Persia. Abdication of Reza Shah the Great. Accession of Mohammad Reza Shah Pahlavi.
1942 Tripartite Treaty of Alliance between Iran, the United Kingdom and the Soviet Union. Second Millspaugh Mission (1942-1945).
1943 Tehran Declaration.
1945 Iran joins the United Nations.
1946 Deliverance of Azerbaijan.
1948 Parliament awards posthumously title "The Great" to Reza Shah.
1951 Nationalization of oil industry.
1955 Iran joins the Baghdad Pact (later known as CENTO).
1967 Coronation of Mohammad Reza Shah Pahlavi, Arya Mehr and Empress Farah.

APPENDIX C

Modern Iranian Historiography*

This paper has been prepared as an aid to be used in the course "History of the Middle East." It is concerned only with the period after the rise of Islam and is based on the sources mentioned in the last part of this essay.

Iranian literature is very rich. This is especially true of poetry and the contributions of the great Sufi writers and Shiite divines. According to Professor Spuler, "Historiography seems to have been of no great importance to pre-Islamic Iranians."[1] After the rise of Islam historians were concerned with *tabaqat*,[2] and *isnad*.[3] The individual writer was of little importance except as a contributor to the transmission of Islamic culture. It has been claimed that medieval Iranian historiography was more limited in scope than its Arabic counterpart. But this is based on a false premise. Actually, many of the Arabic-writing historians of the medieval period were Iranians who wrote in Arabic at this time. This was especially true for the period 642 A.D. to 1255. Among the great Iranian historians who wrote in Arabic one may mention al-Tabari, al-Biruni, al-Baladhuri, and Abu al-Faraj (al-Isfahani).[4]

Iranian writers excelled in writing biographical works.[5] The purpose of the biographer and historian in the Medieval Age was to instruct, divert, but most important to edify. These Iranian historians believed that the purpose of history was more than a collection of stories and traditions. It was the duty of the historian to advise and warn their readers. There were many

---

* This is an abstract from lecture notes of Dr. Kerim Key, The American University, entitled "Modern Iranian Historiography" reproduced with the author's permission.

biographies of saints and mystics (*sufis*). An outstanding example is Attar's *Tazkirat al-awliya*.[6] There were two principal types of biographies. The first were biographic dictionaries of religious sects or orders. Most biographic dictionaries conformed to the pattern of the Muslim-Arabic historiography. They included dates of birth and death, names of teachers, title of works, and journeys and pilgrimages undertaken. Little was mentioned about the political events which they might have participated in. The relevant facts to these biographers were when and where the protagonist lived, his position in the line of transmission (from whom he obtained his knowledge), and what he wrote. An example of a great work was the *Safwatu's-Safa*, a biography of Shaykh Safiyyu'd-Din, a 13th-century saint and founder of the Safavid dynasty.[7] The other type of biography was the history of local families and officials. These works were steeped in provincial particularism. Some writers confined their works to the religious classes, an example being the *Shiraznama* of ibn Zarkub,[8] others wrote about the principal families of certain localities such as Hamdallah Mustawfi's *Tarikh-i Guzida* (Mostofi, *Tarikh-i Gizideh*).[9]

Later historians, of the 18th and 19th centuries, were mostly chroniclers who wrote about the achievements of the Shahs, the court, and sometimes the politics of their times. These works were uncritical narratives. Victories were attributed to the will of Allah and defeats blamed on evil fortune. These historians are readable and even instructive. But they dealt primarily with battles and court intrigues. They neglected social and economic history. While Iranian literature, even in the period of decline, continued to be rich, the history of history was neglected until very recent times. In fact, history-writing was considered a branch of literature until the last few decades.

A few words may be in order about historians of note. For example, Rashid al-Din Tabib (1247-1318) was not only a recorder of events but a medical doctor. Iskandar Munshi wrote about Shah Abbas the Great (1587-1628) in his *Tarikh-i Alam Arya Abbasi* in 1616. Many histories were written by a number of writers. Hasan-i Rumlu completed the rule of Shah Ismail and Tahmasp in *Ahsanu't—Tawarikh* in 1577. One should also mention such sources as the genealogy of the Safavids, *Nasab-nama-i silsila-i Safawiyya*.

For more recent times one can mention the following historians: Abdollah Razi Hamadani, *Tarikh-i Iran.* Tehran, 1938. This is a general History of Iran written in the traditional manner with no documentation or bibliography. It is similar in scope to Sir Percy Sykes, *History of Persia,* but naturally has an Iranian viewpoint. Najaf Qoli Hesam Moezzi, *Tarikh-i siyasiyi Iran va donya,* Tehran, 1927, deals with Iran's relations with Russia and Britain to 1921. Mahmud Mahmud, *Tarikh-i ravabeti siyasiyi Iran va Inglis dar qarna nuzdahome miladi,* Tehran, 1930, is a detailed 10 volume study of Iranian diplomatic history in the 19th century, and is well documented based on Iranian, British, and French sources. While this work is critical of the British, it is a most thorough and comprehensive work.

The history of the Iranian Revolution and Constitutionalism is a subject of interest to Iranian historians as well as to others.[10] There is a valuable work by Mehdi Malekzadeh, *Tarikh-i inqelab va mashrutiyat-i Iran* in 7 volumes. A biographical study of Mirza Taqi Khan (also known as Amir Nezam, Amir Kabir, and Atabaki Azam) a 19th century Prime Minister who opposed the British and became a national hero is interesting reading. It is written by an Iranian diplomat, Fereydoun Adamiyat and is entitled *Amir Kabir va Iran ya varaqi az tarikh-i siyasi Iran* in two volumes (Amir Kabir and Iran or a page from the Political History of Iran).[14]

Until recently most writers of histories were literary men, officials, and gentlemen of leisure. History and geography were generally taught together. In the last two decades a well-established historical profession has emerged as part of the modernization of Iran. Reza Shah Pahlavi stimulated the study of ancient Iran and great interest was shown about the Achaemenid, Sassanid, and Safavid periods of Iranian greatness. Under the leadership of Mohammad Reza Shah Pahlavi, further progress has been achieved in the field of history-writing. The Shah himself has written a *History of Reza Shah the Great.* There are now eight universities in Iran. The result is a new flowering of Iranian scholarship.

An aspect of modernization has been the growing sentiment of nationalism which has characterized the writings of most recent Iranian historical writers. Some Iranian historians have

91

stated that historiography, historical method, and the philosophy of history have been neglected in the past, and greater efforts are needed to develop modern historical techniques. This is also true of Turkish, Arabic, and Pakistani historians of the last century and last generation, but rapid strides are being made in modern scholarship in all the Muslim lands as programs of modernization advance in every field of endeavor including modern scholarship.

The most useful sources for a study of modern Iranian intellectual and social history is Edward G. Browne, *History of Persian Literature in Modern Times 1500-1924* (Cambridge University Press, 1924). There are important chapters by specialists on Iran in Bernard Lewis and P. M. Holt, *eds., Historians of the Middle East* (Oxford University Press, 1962). These include: Bertold Spuler, "The Evolution of Persian Historiography," Mujtaba Minovi, "The Persian Historian Bayhaqi," Ann K. S. Lambton, "Persian Biographic Literature." J. R. Walsh, "The Historiography of Ottoman-Safavid Relations," M. E. Yapp, "Two British Historians and Persia," G. E. Wheeler, "Soviet Writing on Persia from 1906 to 1946," and Firuz Kazemzadeh, "Iranian Historiography." Kazemzadeh has an article entitled "Recent Iranian Historiography," in *Middle Eastern Affairs*, October, 1956. A good bibliographical source on Iranian affairs is Elwell-Sutton, *A Guide to Iranian Area Study* (Ann Arbor: Michigan, ACLS, 1952).

FOOTNOTES

1. B. Spuler, "The Evolution of Persian History," in *Historians of the Middle East,* p. 126. See also R. C. Dentan, *ed., The Idea of History in the Ancient Near East,* Yale, 1955.
2. *Tabagat,* classes or classification, was used for collections of biographies arranged by categories or classes according to the particular point of view which the author wished to emphasize.
3. *Isnad,* "chain" of authorities were quoted. The recorders of the sayings and acts of the Prophet Muhammad were persons of sound knowledge. Biographies were classified by the place each transmitter held in the "chain" which linked him with the original source of information, and established the degree of his trustworthiness.
4. One of the earliest of historians of Iran was al-Dinawari (895 A.D.). Al-Tabari (d. 923 A.D.) was a great historian and al-Baladhuri (d. 892) is revered in Muslim history. Abu al-Faraj (d. 967) came from Isfahan which has produced great thinkers and artists. Hamzeh is

known for his *Selselat-oz-Zahab* (Prairies of Gold), and al-Biruni (d. 1048) was a prolific writer. *Zein-ol-Akhbar* and *Tarikh-i Beihaghi* were written in 1051 and 1077 during the Ghaznavid era. Also worth mentioning are: *Mowjam-ot-Tavarikh* (1126); Ravandi's *Rahat os-Sodur* (1213); Joweini's *Jahangosha,* a history of the Mongols (1260); *Tarikh-i Vassaf* (1312); *Jame'ot-Tavarikh* (1318); and *Tarikh-i Gozideh* (1310) by Mostowfi, a remarkable work. Yazdi composed his history of Tamerlane in 1482. Khavandamir's *Habib-os-Siar* is one of the greatest post-Mongol works. During the Safavid period, *Alam Arya Abbasi* was written, while Karim Khan and Nadir Shah had their own historians. There were also historians of most important cities, especially Isfahan and Kerman.

5. See Ann K. Lambton, "Persian Biographic Literature," in *Historians of the Middle East,* pp. 141-151.
6. Attar in his preface to his *Tazkirat al-awliya* explains why he wrote on the life of the saints. He stated that important posts were in the hands of bad people, while holy men had been forgotten.
7. *Safwatu's Safa.* Bombay, 1911.
8. *Shiraznama* was completed in 1344.
9. *Tarikh-i Guzida* deals with families of Qazwin. It was completed in 1330.
10. See Edward G. Browne, *The Persian Revolution of 1905-1909,* Cambridge University, 1910.
11. Also author of *Bahrein Islands.* New York: Praeger, 1955.
12. There are many histories of Iran but space will not allow listing as many as one would desire. Here are a few worth noting: *Tarikh-i ba'd Nadiriyya;* Leiden, 1891; Nizamu'l Islam of Kirman, *Tarikh-i Bidari-yi Iraniyan,* 1910 (History of the awakening of the Iranians); and Ali Rida, *Tarikh-i Zandiyya,* Leiden, 1888 (Post Safavid period).

APPENDIX D

The Iranian Constitution

To His Highness the Prime Minister

WHEREAS, God Most High, Glorious in His State, hath entrusted to Our capable hands the direction of the progress and prosperity of the well-protected realms of Iran, and hath constituted Our Royal Personage the Guardian of the Rights of all the people of Iran and of all Our loyal subjects,

THEREFORE, on this occasion when we are determined that, for the welfare and security of all the people of Iran, and for the strengthening and consolidation of the foundations of the State, such reforms as are suitable in the different departments of the State and of the country shall gradually be effected. We have decided that a National Consultative Assembly shall be formed and constituted in Tehran, the capital of Iran, with deputies to be elected by the following classes of people: the Princes, the ulema (Moslem clergy), the Qajar family, the nobles and notables, the landowners, the merchants and tradesmen. The Assembly shall carry out the requisite deliberations and investigations on all necessary subjects connected with important affairs of the State and the country and the public interest; and it shall render the necessary help and assistance to Our Cabinet of Ministers in such reforms as are designed to promote the happiness and well-being of Iran; and it shall, with complete confidence and security, through the first Lord of the State (the Prime Minister) submit to Us its views for the good of the State and in the interest of all the people of the country so that these, having been duly signed by Us, may be carried into effect.

It is evident that, in accordance with the August Rescript, you will from this date arrange and prepare regulations governing this Assembly and the means necessary to organize it, with the approval of Deputies to be elected and with Imperial sanction, so that with the help of God Most High this Assembly may be inaugurated to uphold the cause of justice, to proceed with the necessary reforms and enforce the tenets of the holy Shari'at.

We likewise decree that you shall publish and proclaim the text of this August Rescript, so that all the people of Iran may be duly informed of Our good intentions, which are entirely for the progress of the Government and the People of Iran, and so that they may, with tranquil minds, engage in prayer for the State and for this everlasting blessing.

Given under Our Hand in the Saheb-Qaraniya Palace on the fourteenth day of Jomadi-os-Sani in the lunar year of the Hejira 1324 (August 5, 1906) in the eleventh year of Our Reign.

(Signed by) Mozaffar-ed-Din Shah Qajar

✔ ✔ ✔

THE CONSTITUTIONAL LAW

Of December 30, 1906 (Zulqa'deh A.H. 1324)
In The Name of God, The Compassionate,
The Most Merciful!

WHEREAS, by Imperial Firman (decree) dated the fourteenth of Jomadi-os-Sani A.H. 1324 (August 5, 1906) We ordered that a National Council be set up to promote the progress and happiness of Our kingdom and people, strengthen the foundations of Our Government, and carry out the Sacred Law of His Holiness the last of all Prophets, may the praise of Allah be upon Him and His Posterity.

WHEREAS, by virtue of the fundamental principle (therein laid down), that every individual in the realm has the right to participate in approving and superintending the affairs of the commonwealth, each person according to his rank, We have left it to the judgment of the nation to choose the Members of this Assembly by popular election.

95

THEREFORE, the National Consultative Assembly having now opened in accordance with Our sacred designs, We lay down hereunder the principles and articles of the Fundamental Law regulating the National Consultative Assembly, its duties and functions, its province and its relations with the various departments of the State.

✓   ✓   ✓

THE ORGANIZATION OF THE NATIONAL CONSULTATIVE ASSEMBLY

Article 1. The National Consultative Assembly (Majlis) is established and constituted in accordance with the Imperial decree of August 5, 1906.

Article 2. The National Consultative Assembly represents all the inhabitants of the kingdom of Iran associated in the political and economic affairs of the country.

Article 3. The National Consultative Assembly is composed of members elected at Tehran and in the provinces; it meets in Tehran.

Article 4.* The number of Deputies in the National Consultative Assembly (Majlis) for the capital and for the provinces shall be two hundred, and after every ten years, in case the population of the country increases in any constituency, one Deputy shall be added for every one hundred thousand persons according to official census.

Appointment of (Deputies to) constituencies shall be in accordance with special law.**

Article 5.* The term of office in the National Consultative Assembly is four full years and it includes the Nineteenth Term. Prior to the expiration of the period, new elections shall be held according to the law. The beginning of each term shall

---

* This amendment passed on May 16, 1957, by the Senate and National Consultative Assembly in a joint meeting of Congress, in conformity with the last portion of the Article annexed to the Supplementary Constitutional Law.

** Translator's Note: The electoral law of September 17, 1906, divided the electors into six classes—princes and members of the royal family, professors and students, nobles, officials, merchants, and farmers. These classes were abolished by the electoral law of July 1, 1909, which substituted election in two stages.

be from the date of the approval of credentials of more than half the Deputies. There is nothing to prevent the re-election of former Deputies.

Article 6.* The National Consultative Assembly convenes after two-thirds of the Deputies of the National Consultative Assembly are present in the capital.

Article 7.* The Assembly (Majlis) may proceed with deliberations in the presence of any number that may attend the meeting. However, when a vote is taken, the presence of more than half the Deputies present in the capital is necessary. And a majority of votes is obtained when more than half the members present in the meeting vote for or against the matter (under discussion).

Article 8.* The duration of vacations and sessions of the National Consultative Assembly shall be decided by an internal ruling of its own, and after the summer vacation the Assembly shall be reopened to resume its work on the fourteenth of Mizan (this year October 6) which corresponds with the anniversary of its first opening.

Article 9. During vacations the National Consultative Assembly may be recalled to hold extraordinary session.

Article 10. At the time of its opening the National Consultative Assembly shall present an address to His Imperial Majesty the Shah, and shall have the honour of hearing the reply of His Imperial Majesty.

Article 11. The members of the National Consultative Assembly, when they enter the Assembly for the first time, must take the following oath and subscribe to it:

"We, the undersigned, invoke God as our witness and swear on the Qur'an that, as long as the rights of Parliament and its members are respected and carried out in accordance with this law, we shall most faithfully, uprightly and diligently fulfill to the utmost of our powers the duties which have been conferred upon us, and that we shall remain loyal and truthful to our just, obeyed and honoured Sovereign, His Imperial Majesty; that we will not betray the institution of His kingdom (the foundations of His Throne) and the rights of the people, and that we will consider nothing that is inconsistent with the interests of the Government and the Iranian people."

Article 12. No one may molest a member of the National Consultative Assembly on any ground or excuse without the knowledge and approval of the National Consultative Assembly; and if by chance a member shall have openly committed a crime, felony or misdemeanor and shall have been arrested in *flagrante delicto,* no penalty can be inflicted upon him without the Assembly having been advised.

Article 13. The discussions of the Assembly must be public in order that their results may be put into effect; journalists and visitors have the right to attend debates and to follow them in accordance with the internal regulations of the Assembly, but not the right to speak. All discussions of the National Consultative Assembly may be published in the press, on condition that they are not modified in form or meaning, so that all may know the discussions and the course of events. Whoever thinks he can give a useful opinion may publish it in the press, so that nothing shall remain hidden or unknown. Thus all newspapers, so long as their contents are not contrary to any of the fundamental principles of the State or the nation shall be at liberty to print useful subjects of public interest, Parliamentary debates and opinions of citizens on these discussions; at the same time, anyone who publishes something in the press or other publications contrary to the foregoing and from personal motives, or is guilty of libel, shall be liable to arraignment and trial and shall be punished in accordance with the law.

Article 14. The National Consultative Assembly, by a special regulation, entitled "Internal Regulations" (Rules of Procedure), shall regulate its own affairs, such as the election of its President and vice-President, Secretaries and other employees, the procedure for discussions, the formation of committees, etc.

✓   ✓   ✓

The Duties, Sphere of Authority and Rights of the National Consultative Assembly

Article 15. The National Consultative Assembly shall have the right in all questions to examine and discuss, in all sincerity and truth, ruling by the majority, in complete security and confidence, whatever it considers in the interests of the country and the nation; after they have been approved by the Senate, decisions must be submitted to the Sovereign by the head of the Government and put into effect after receiving Royal approval.

Article 16. All laws necessary for the consolidation of the foundations of the State and of the kingdom (the Throne) for the regulation of the affairs of the country and for the establishment of ministries, must be approved by the National Consultative Assembly.

Article 17. The National Consultative Assembly shall, when occasion arises, draft such bills as may be necessary for the creation, modification, completion or repeal of existing laws. They will come into force when they have been approved by the Senate and signed by His Majesty.

Article 18. The regulation of financial questions, adjustment of the budget, changes in taxation, the acceptance or rejection of duties, charges and new assessments instituted by the Government, must be with the approval of the National Consultative Assembly.

Article 19. The National Consultative Assembly, after approval by the Senate, shall have the right to call upon the Government to put into effect any decisions taken to make tax reforms and to facilitate relations with the Governmental authorities in the administrative division of the country and the provinces and to define the limits of Governorships.*

Article 20. The budget of each Ministry must be completed during the second half of each year for the following year and be ready fifteen days before New Year's Day (Noruz festival).**

Article 21. Whenever a new law is necessary to supplement the basic laws of the Ministries or to amend or repeal existing laws, this law shall be made with the approval of the National Consultative Assembly, whether the need for it shall have been suggested by the Assembly or by responsible Ministers.

Article 22. The approval of the National Consultative Assembly is necessary for all transfers or sales of the revenues or

---

* The Persian wording of this Article is rather ambiguous. It apparently conflicts with Article 46 hereunder.
** The Iranian New Year, corresponding to March 21 or 22.

properties of the State or the country, and for all modifications of the frontiers of the country.

Article 23. The State cannot grant any concession for the creation of any kind of company and public partnership without asking authorization from the National Consultative Assembly.

Article 24. The conclusion of treaties and agreements, the granting of commercial, industrial, agricultural or other concessions (monopolies), whether the concessionaire is a national or a foreigner, must be authorized by the National Consultative Assembly, except for treaties which it would be in the interests of the State and the nation to keep secret.***

Article 25. No State loan at home or abroad may be raised without the knowledge and approval of the National Consultative Assembly.

Article 26. The construction of railways and chaussée roads, whether at the expense of the State, or at the expense of national or foreign corporations and companies, requires the approval of the National Consultative Assembly.

Article 27. Whenever the National Consultative Assembly observes a violation or negligence in the application of the laws, it shall notify the Minister responsible who shall provide the necessary explanation.

Article 28. Should any Minister, contrary to one of the laws enacted and approved (signed) by His Majesty, fraudulently issue written or verbal orders on His Majesty's authority and use such orders as an excuse for his negligence and lack of attention, he shall, according to the law, be responsible to His Sacred Majesty personally.

Article 29. Should a Minister be unable to give a satisfactory account of any affair according to the laws approved (signed) by His Majesty, and should it be agreed that he has acted contrary to the law or that he has transgressed the limits imposed (on him), the Assembly shall request His Majesty to dismiss him; and should his treason be proved before the Court of Justice, he shall no longer be eligible for public office.

Article 30. The Assembly has the right, whenever it considers necessary, to present a petition to His Majesty, through the

***Translator's Note: See Article 52 of the Supplementary Constitutional Law of October 8, 1907.

100

medium of a committee composed of the President and six members chosen by the six classes of deputies. His Majesty shall be requested through the Minister of Court to grant an audience to the committee.

Article 31. The Ministers have the right to attend the sessions of the National Consultative Assembly, to occupy places reserved for them, to listen to the debates, and if necessary, after asking permission from the President, to give any explanations that may be necessary for the careful examination of the questions discussed.

✓ ✓ ✓

On the Presentation of Proposals to the National Consultative Assembly

Article 32. Anyone may address in writing his requests, complaints or criticisms to the Petitions Office of the Assembly; if the matter concerns the Assembly, it shall itself make the necessary reply; if it concerns one of the Ministries the Assembly shall forward it to the Ministry for examination and sufficient reply.

Article 33. New laws that appear necessary shall be prepared and critically revised in the Ministries responsible and shall be presented to the Assembly by the Minister concerned or by the Prime Minister. After having been voted by the Assembly and having received the Royal signature, they shall be put into force.

Article 34. The President of the Assembly may, if necessary, personally or at the request of ten members of the Assembly or of one of the Ministers, summon a secret meeting from which newspapermen and spectators shall be excluded, or may hold a secret conference composed of a certain selected number of members, to which the other members shall not be admitted. However the decisions of the secret conference shall not be effective unless three-quarters of the members elected are present and take part in it and unless the decision shall have been taken by a majority of votes. If the proposal is not accepted by the secret conference, it shall not be presented to the Assembly and shall be passed over in silence.

Article 35. If the secret meeting takes place at the request of the President of the Assembly, he may inform the public of such parts of the debate as he may think fit; but if it is held at the request of a Minister, the disclosure of deliberations depends on the permission of that Minister.

Article 36. Any Minister may withdraw from the Assembly a proposal put forward by him, at any stage of the discussions, unless the proposal shall have been made at the request of the Assembly; in that case the withdrawal of the proposal depends on the assent of the Assembly.

Article 37. If a bill introduced by a Minister is not accepted by the Assembly, it shall be returned to the Minister with the Assembly's observations. The Minister concerned may accept or reject the Assembly's criticisms and present the bill again to the Assembly.

Article 38. The members of the Assembly must plainly and clearly declare their rejection or acceptance of the proposals, and no one may influence their vote by promises or threat; the rejection or acceptance must be made in such a way as to be perceivable by newspaper reporters and spectators, that is to say, shown by outward sign, such as white and blue voting papers, or the like.

✓   ✓   ✓

PRESENTATION OF PROPOSALS EMANATING FROM THE NATIONAL CONSULTATIVE ASSEMBLY

Article 39. If a proposal is presented by a member of the National Consultative Assembly, it may only be debated if at least fifteen members approve its discussion. In that case, it shall be presented in writing to the President, who may have it first examined by a Committee of Inquiry.

Article 40. If the bill mentioned in Article 39 concerns one of the responsible Ministers, the Assembly must notify this Minister so that he may be represented in person, if possible, or by his Under-Secretary and may take part in the debate and discussions held in the Chamber or in the Committee of Inquiry. A copy of the bill and any supplement must be forwarded to the responsible Minister ten days to a month before the beginning of the debate, except in the case of urgent matters; in the same way the date of the debate must be fixed in advance.

After the matter has been examined in the presence of the responsible Minister, and if it is adopted by a majority of votes of the Assembly, it shall be given in an official written form to the Minister for appropriate action.

Article 41. Whenever the responsible Minister does not agree with the proposal made by the Assembly, he must explain his reasons and convince the Assembly.

Article 42. When the National Consultative Assembly demands an explanation of any matter, the Minister concerned is bound to reply. This reply must not be delayed unreasonably, except in the case of matters the secrecy of which for a certain period is demanded by the national interest; after this period, however, the responsible Minister is bound to disclose the matter to the Assembly.

✓   ✓   ✓

On the Conditions Relating to the Formation of the Senate

Article 43. Another Assembly called the Senate and composed of sixty members shall be formed; after formation, its sessions shall be held at the same time as those of the National Consultative Assembly (Majlis).*

Article 44. The Regulations (Rules of Procedure) of the Senate must be approved by the National Consultative Assembly.

Article 45. The members of the Senate shall be elected from amongst the well-informed, discerning, devout and respected persons of the country. Thirty members shall be nominated by His Imperial Majesty, fifteen from Tehran and fifteen from the provinces. Thirty members shall be elected by the people, fifteen from Tehran and fifteen from the provinces.

Article 46. After the formation of the Senate, all proposals shall be approved by the two assemblies; if the proposals emanate from the Senate or from the Cabinet they must first be critically revised and corrected in the Senate and approved by a majority of votes; they shall then be submitted for the

---

* See Articles 29 and 32 of the Election Law for the Senate approved by the Majlis on May 4, 1949, and promulgated by His Imperial Majesty on May 18, 1949, on the six year term of the Senate.

approval of the National Consultative Assembly. However, proposals emanating from the National Consultative Assembly shall on the contrary go from this Assembly to the Senate except for financial questions, which are reserved to the National Consultative Assembly. The decision of the National Consultative Assembly on these questions shall be brought to the notice of the Senate so that the Senate may communicate its observations to the Assembly; but the latter is free, after due examination, to accept or reject these observations.

Article 47. As long as the Senate is not in session, proposals shall be voted on by the National Consultative Assembly alone; after receiving the Royal signature, they shall be put into effect.

Article 48. (As amended).** The King may dissolve the National Consultative Assembly or the Senate separately or at the same time. In each case, when one or both Chambers are dissolved by Imperial decree, the reason for the dissolution must be mentioned in the decree which shall also provide for new elections.

The new elections must begin within a month after the date of the decree and the new Majlis or both new Houses must convene within three months after the same date.

** As amended by the Constituent Assembly of May 8, 1949 (Ordibehesht 18, 1328). For convenience of reference the repealed Article is also quoted hereinbelow in translation:

Article 48 (repealed). Whenever a proposal emanating from a Minister shall, after critical revision and correction by the Senate, be submitted to the National Consultative Assembly and rejected by the said Assembly, if it is of sufficient importance, a third assembly shall be formed by members of the Senate and the National Consultative Assembly, elected in equal numbers by members of both Houses, to study the question at issue. The resulting decision of this (third) assembly shall be read in the National Consultative Assembly. If an agreement is reached, well and good; if not, the matter shall be submitted for the consideration of His Majesty. If his Majesty approves the vote of the National Consultative Assembly, the proposal shall be put into effect; if He does not approve it, He shall order a fresh discussion and careful examination. If again no agreement is reached, and the Senate, by a majority of two-thirds of its members, approves the dissolution of the National Consultative Assembly, and the Cabinet separately confirms this dissolution a Royal Decree will be issued for the dissolution of the National Consultative Assembly, and in the same decree orders will be given for new elections. The people shall, however, have the right to reelect the former Deputies.

The new Chamber, thus constituted after the dissolution (of its predecessor), will sit for the term of a new legislature and not for the time remaining from the dissolved legislature.

The new Chamber or Chambers may not be dissolved for the same reason (as the preceding one or ones).

When the Senate and National Consultative Assembly fail to come to an agreement on a project of law or bill which has been sent twice from one Chamber to the other, a joint Committee made up of an equal number of members from the two Chambers shall study the differences and present its report to both Chambers. If the Senate and National Consultative Assembly approve the report of the joint Committee, the law in question shall be presented for the Imperial signature.

If the Chambers do not agree with the report of the joint Committee, the dispute shall be submitted to His Imperial Majesty. And if His Imperial Majesty approves the decision of the National Consultative Assembly he will order it to be put into effect, otherwise the question will be deferred for six months and, whenever expedient, the proposal may come up at the expiration of this period in the form of a new measure or bill in either House.

Article 48 and all other Articles of the Constitution dated 14 Zulqa'deh, 1324, lunar year of the Hejira (31 December, 1906), and its supplement which may be inconsistent with this Article are annulled.

The above Article was approved by the Constituent Assembly in its session of May 8, 1949 (Ordibehesht 18, 1328).

(Signed) MOHAMMAD SADEQ TABATABAI
President of the Constituent Assembly.

Article 49. Those (members who are) newly elected from Tehran must assemble within one month and those elected from the provinces within three months. When those who are elected from the capital are assembled, the Assembly shall convene and commence its work, but shall not discuss the question in dispute before the arrival of those elected from the provinces. If, with all its members present, the New Assembly confirms the previous decision by a full majority, His Imperial Majesty shall approve the decision of the National Consultative Assembly and shall order it to be put into force.

Article 50. The renewal of the elections cannot be ordered more than once during each electoral (legislative) term which is two years.*

Article 51. It is laid down that the kings of our posterity shall regard as a duty of their reign of observance of these principles which We have established and put into force to consolidate the foundations of the State, strengthen the basis of the Throne and protect the institutions of justice and the welfare of the people.

In the name of God Almighty, these Fundamental Laws of the National Consultative Assembly and the Senate, consisting of fifty-one Articles, are all correct.

December 30, 1906 (Zulga'deh 14, 1324 A.H.)
(Signed) 1. MOZAFFAR-ED-DIN SHAH
2. MOHAMMAD ALI QAJAR,
Heir Apparent,
(afterwards Shah,
later deposed)
3. MOSHIR-ED-DOWLEH.

SUPPLEMENTARY CONSTITUTIONAL LAW OF OCTOBER 8, 1907

In The Name of God, The Compassionate, The Most Merciful!

The following clauses complete the fundamental law of the Constitution of the State of Iran, according to the Fundamental Law signed on August 6, 1906 (Zulqa'deh 14, 1324 A.H.) by the late Mozaffar-ed-Din Shah Qajar, may the light of God shine upon His grave!

GENERAL PRINCIPLES

Article 1. The State religion of Iran is Islam, according to the true Ja'fariya doctrine, recognizing twelve Imams. The Shah of Iran must profess and propagate this faith.

---

* See Article 5 of the Constitution as amended on May 16, 1957, extending the legislative term of the Majlis to four years.

Article 2. At no time may the enactments of the sacred National Consultative Assembly, which has been constituted with the aid and favour of His Holiness the Imam of the Age (Imam Mahdi, the Twelfth Imam) may God immortalize His reign! and under the supervision of the learned doctors of theology, may God increase their number! and by the whole Iranian people, be at variance with the sacred precepts of Islam and the laws laid down by His Holiness the Best of Mankind (the Prophet), may the blessings of God rest upon Him and His descendants! It is plain that the learned doctors of theology, may God prolong their beneficient lives! are charged with the duty of determining any contradiction between the laws made by the Assembly and the principles of Islam. It is, therefore solemnly laid down that at all times there shall be constituted as follows a body of at least five devout doctors of Islamic law and jurisprudence who shall at the same time be conversant with the exigencies of their age: The most learned doctors of theology in Islam who are recognized as such and whose example is followed by the Shi'ites shall nominate to the National Consultative Assembly twenty doctors of theology possessing the above qualifications; the members of the Assembly shall choose five or more of them, according to circumstances, by a unanimous vote or by drawing lots, and shall recognize them as members so that they may carefully discuss and deliberate the bills proposed in both Houses, and reject (veto) any that contravene the holy principles of Islam, so that they shall not become law; the decisions of this body of doctors of theology on this point shall be followed and obeyed. This clause may not be modified until the Advent of the Imam of the Age, may God hasten His reappearance!*

Article 3. The frontiers of Iran and the boundaries of the provinces, districts and counties cannot be changed except by law.

Article 4. The capital of Iran is Tehran.

Article 5. The official colours of the flag of Iran are green, white and red. The emblem is a Lion and Sun.

Article 6. The lives and property of foreign nations resident

---

* Translator's Note: i.e., until the Twelfth Imam shall return to establish the reign of perfect justice.

in Iranian territory are safe and protected, except as subject to the laws of the country.

Article 7. The principles of the Constitution may not be suspended either wholly or in part.

✐ ✐ ✐

The Rights of the Iranian People

Article 8. The inhabitants of the Empire of Iran shall enjoy equal rights before the law.

Article 9. Individuals are protected and safeguarded against offenses of any kind against their lives, their property, their homes and their honour. No one may be molested, except in accordance with the laws of the land.

Article 10. Except in the cases of crimes, misdemeanors and serious offenses, no one may be summarily arrested without an order signed by the President of the Court of Justice in conformity with the law, even in this case the accused must immediately, or at latest within twenty-four hours, be informed and notified of the charge against him.

Article 11. No one may be removed from the court which must render judgment on his case and forced to another tribunal.

Article 12. No penalty may be decreed or carried out except in accordance with the law.

Article 13. Everyone's house and dwelling is protected and safeguarded. No one may enter forcibly into any dwelling except by order of and in conformity with the law.

Article 14. No Iranian may be exiled, or forbidden or compelled to reside in any particular place, except in cases specified by law.

Article 15. No one may be dispossessed of his property, except in cases authorized by religious law, and then only after the fair value (of such property) has been determined and paid.

Article 16. The confiscation of the real property, goods and chattels (or possessions) of individuals as a penalty is forbidden except in conformity with the law.

Article 17. The dispossession of any grounds whatever of property-owners or possessors of the real property and possessions is forbidden except by order of the law.

Article 18. The study and teaching of science, education and art are free, except as prohibited by religious law.

Article 19. The institution of schools at the expense of the State and the nation and compulsory education shall take place according to the law relating to the Ministry of Education. All higher and primary schools are placed under the supreme direction and supervision of the Ministry of Education.

Article 20. All publications are free, except heretical books and materials hurtful to the perspicuous religion (of Islam). The censorship of publications is forbidden. If, however, anything is found in them contrary to the Press Law, the publisher or writer shall be punished in conformity with that Law. If the writer is known and living in Iran, the publisher, printer and distributor shall be immune from molestation.

Article 21. Societies and gatherings which do not give rise to religious or civil disorders and are not prejudicial to public order are free throughout the country, but their members may not carry arms, and they must obey the regulations laid down by the law on this subject. Meetings in streets and public squares must conform to police regulations.

Article 22. All postal correspondence is inviolable and immune from confiscation or disclosure except in accordance with the law.

Article 23. It is forbidden to divulge or detain telegrams without the permission of the owner, except in the cases provided for by the law.

Article 24. Foreign nationals may acquire Iranian nationality. The acceptance, continuation or withdrawal of their naturalization are the subject of a separate law.

Article 25. Authorization is not necessary for the prosecution of State officials on account of faults in the exercise of their duties except Ministers, in whose case special laws on this subject must be observed.

✓   ✓   ✓

POWERS OF THE STATE

Article 26. The powers of the State are derived from the nation. The method of exercising these powers is regulated by the constitutional law.

Article 27. The powers of the state are divided into three parts:

1) The legislative power, whose special function is to make and modify (recense) the laws. This power is derived from His Imperial Majesty, the National Consultative Assembly and the Senate. Each of these three sources has the right to introduce laws, but any project of law becomes law only when it is not at variance with religious principles of Islam, and is approved by the two Houses and signed by His Imperial Majesty. However, the enactment and approval of laws concerning the revenues and expenditure of the country are especially reserved to the National Consultative Assembly.

The explanation and interpretation of the laws are amongst the special functions of the National Consultative Assembly.

2) The judicial power, whose function is to determine the right, is reserved to the religious courts in matters relating to the Shari'at (Islamic law) and to the judiciary (temporal courts) in secular matters.

3) The executive power is reserved to the King, that is to say, the laws and decrees shall be carried out by the Ministers and State officials in the august name of His Imperial Majesty in such manner as the Law defines.

Article 28. The three above-mentioned powers shall always remain separate and distinct from one another.

Article 29. The special interests of each province, district and county shall, with the approval of provincial, district and county councils, be arranged and regulated in accordance with special laws.

✓   ✓   ✓

RIGHTS OF THE MEMBERS OF THE TWO HOUSES

Article 30. The deputies and senators represent the whole nation and not only the particular classes of the people or the provinces, districts or counties which have elected them.

Article 31. No one may be a member of both Houses at the same time.

Article 32. If one of the members of one or the other House*
is employed with a salary in one of the departments of the
Government, he shall cease to be a member of the Assembly.
To return to the Assembly as a member, he must resign his
Government post and be reelected by the people.

Article 33. Each of the two Assemblies has the right to
investigate and examine any affair of the State.

Article 34. The discussions of the Senate shall be ineffective
when the National Consultative Assembly is not in session.**

✔   ✔   ✔

RIGHTS OF THE THRONE IN IRAN

Article 35. The Sovereignty is a trust confided, by the Grace
of God, to the person of the King by the nation.

Article 36. (As amended December 12, 1925). The Constitutional Monarchy of Iran is vested by the people through the

---

* Translator's Note: The term *Vokala* (plural of Vakil) has been used
in Article 30 supra to apply to members of both houses. The same term
has been again used in Article 32, both of which fall under the heading
"The Rights of members of both Houses." It has, therefore, been trans-
lated here as "members of one or the other House."

With regard to the Deputies, the National Consultative Assembly
passed a law on July 14, 1927 (Tirmah 22, 1306), further clarifying this
Constitutional provision. Here follows a translation of that Law:

"Article 1.—All Chiefs of Government Offices are deprived of the right
to be elected as Deputy to the National Consultative Assembly from the
place where they have been assigned to duty, and also Cabinet Ministers
and their Under Secretaries from all parts of the country at the time of
elections.

"Article 2.—Until the expiration of any legislative term, the Deputies
of the National Consultative Assembly may not accept any Government
office with salary unless they should have resigned as Deputies three months
before they accept such (Government) service."

With regard to Senators the Senate adopted the following resolution on
October 23, 1951 (Aban 1, 1330) which forms an annex to the Internal
Regulations (the Rules of Procedure) in the Senate:

"The acceptance by Senators of Government offices such as Cabinet
Minister, Governor General and Ambassador shall hereafter be tantamount
to resignation from their seats in the Senate."

** Literally "during the period of dissolution of the National Consultative Assembly."

Constituent Assembly in the person of His Imperial Majesty Reza Shah Pahlavi and his male descendants in succession.***

Article 37. (As amended December 12, 1925). The (right of) succession to Throne shall rest with the eldest son of the King, whose mother must be of Iranian origin.* If the King has no male child, the nomination of the Crown Prince shall be made at the suggestion of the King and with the approval of the National Consultative Assembly, on condition that this Crown Prince shall not be a member of the Qajar family; but at any time, is a son is born to the King, he shall be Crown Prince by right.

Article 38. (As amended December 12, 1925). In the event of the transfer of the Throne, the Crown Prince shall personally perform the functions of Royalty when he has reached twenty years of age (to be calculated on the basis of the solar calendar). If he has not reached that age, a Regent, who shall not

*** The three articles which were repealed by the Constituent Assembly on December 12, 1925, were as follows:

"Article 36 (repealed): The Constitutional Monarchy of Iran is vested in the person of His Imperial Majesty Sultan Mohammad Ali Shah Qajar, may God prolong his sovereignty, and in his heirs, generation after generation.

"Article 37 (repealed: The succession to the Throne, when there are more than one son, passes to the eldest son of the King whose mother is a Princess of Iranian origin. In case the King should have no male issue, the eldest (person) in the Royal Family who is next of kin shall succeed to the Throne. If, however, in the hypothetical case mentioned above, male heirs should subsequently be born to the King, the succession will *de jure* revert to such heir.

"Article 38 (repealed): At the time of the transfer of the Throne the Crown Prince can undertake in person the functions of the Throne (only when he has attained the age of eighteen years). If he has not reached this age, a Regent shall be chosen with the approval of the National Consultative Assembly and the Senate in joint session, until such time as the Crown Prince shall attain the age of eighteen years.

* This Article was interpreted as follows by Act of the Majlis, approved on November 5, 1938 (Aban 14, 1317), so far as it concerns the words "Iranian Origin": *Single Article*. By "mother of Iranian Origin" mentioned in Article 3 of the Supplementary Constitutional Law mother is meant who is accordance with Paragraph 2 of Article 976 of the Civil Code is of Iranian ancestry, or mother who prior to marriage with the King or with the Crown Prince of Iran should have been granted Iranian quality, as required by the High interests of the country, on the recommendation of the Government, with the approval of the National Consultative Assembly and by decree of the reigning Sovereign.

be of the Qajar family, shall be elected by the National Consultative Assembly.

Article 39. No King may ascend the Throne unless, prior to his coronation, he appears before the National Consultative Assembly, and in the presence of the members of the Assembly, the Senate and the Cabinet, he shall have taken the following oath:

> "I call upon God Almighty as witness, and I swear upon the Glorious Word of God (the Qar'an) and upon all that is respected by God to exert all my efforts to preserve the independence of Iran, to protect the frontiers of the country and the rights of the nation, to be the guardian of the Constitutional Law of Iran and to reign accordingly and in conformity with established laws, and to endeavor to promote the Ja'fari doctrine of the (Shi'ah) sect of Twelve Imams, and in all my deeds and actions I shall remember God, Most Glorious as being present and watchful, and shall have no aim but the happiness and greatness of the State and the Nation of Iran. And I seek the aid of God, whose help is begged (by all) to serve the progress of Iran with success, and I seek the help of the Holy Spirits of the Great Saints of Islam!"

Article 40. Likewise, no one chosen as Regent may assume his functions until he has taken the above oath.

Article 41. In the event of the decease of the King, the National Consultative Assembly and the Senate shall of necessity meet, and the meeting of the two Houses must not be postponed more than ten days after the death of the King.

Article 42. If the term of office of the members of either or both Assemblies expires during the life of the King and if new members have not yet been elected at the time of the King's decease, the old members shall reassemble, and the two Houses shall meet again.

Article 43. The King cannot take charge of another country without the consent and approval of the National Consultative Assembly and the Senate.

Article 44. The King is free of responsibility. The Ministers of State are responsible for all matters to both Chambers.

Article 45. All decrees and rescripts of the King relating

to the affairs of the country shall be put into effect (only) when they have been signed by the responsible Minister who is responsible for the correctness of the contents of the decree and rescript.

Article 46. The Ministers are appointed and dismissed by the decree of the King.

Article 47. It is a prerogative of the King to confer military ranks, decorations and other honorary distinctions in conformity with the law.

Article 48. The nomination of the heads of Government departments, internal or foreign, is the King's right with the approval of the responsible Minister, except where the law provides otherwise. However, the nomination of other officials is not a concern of the King, except as expressly provided by the law.

Article 49.** It is one of the rights of the King to issue decrees and give orders for the enforcement of laws, without ever having the power to delay or postpone their enforcement. If His Majesty the King finds a revision necessary in the laws relating to the financial affairs of the country which are a prerogative of the Nation Consultative Assembly, he shall return the laws to the National Consultative Assembly for reexamination. In case the National Consultative Assembly confirms its previous view by a majority vote of three-fourths of the members present in the Capital, His Imperial Majesty shall sign the law.

Article 50. Commander-in-Chief of all the land and sea forces is the King in person.

Article 51. The declaration of war and the conclusion of peace are functions of the King.

Article 52. Treaties the secrecy of which is essential as provided by Article 24 of the Constitutional Law of December 30, 1906, must as soon as the reasons which necessitated such secrecy cease to exist and the interests and security of the country allow, be brought by the King to the notice of the National Consultative Assembly and the Senate with all necessary explanations.

** This Amendment was passed on May 16, 1957, by the Senate and National Consultative Assembly in a joint meeting of Congress, in conformity with the last portion of the Article annexed to the Supplementary Constitutional Law.

Article 53. The secret clauses of a treaty may not nullify those made public.

Article 54. The King may order an extraordinary meeting of the National Consultative Assembly and the Senate.

Article 55. Money is coined in the name of the King, in conformity with the law.

Article 56. The costs and expenses of the Royal Court shall be determined by law.

Article 57. The prerogatives and powers of the King are only those expressly mentioned in this Constitutional Law.

✓ ✓ ✓

THE MINISTERS

Article 58. No one may be nominated Minister unless he is a Moslem of Iranian origin and is an Iranian subject.

Article 59. The Princes of the first degree—that is to say, the sons, brothers and paternal uncles of the reigning King— may not be nominated as Ministers.

Article 60. The Ministers are responsible to the two Chambers; whenever they are summoned by one of the Houses, they must appear before it, and they must observe the limits of their responsibility in such matters as are committed to their charge.

Article 61. Ministers, besides being individually responsible for the affairs of their own Ministry, are also jointly responsible for general matters before the two Chambers, and are collectively bound for one another's actions.

Article 62. The number of Ministers shall be fixed by law according to need.

Article 63. The title of honorary Minister is strictly forbidden.

Article 64. The Ministers may not invoke written or verbal orders of the King in order to disavow their responsibilities.

Article 65. The National Consultative Assembly or the Senate can call Ministers to account and bring them to trial.

Article 66. The responsibility of Ministers and punishments to which they may be liable shall be determined by law.

Article 67. When the National Consultative Assembly or the Senate, by a full majority of votes, declares itself dissatisfied with the Cabinet or a Minister, the Cabinet or Minister shall be considered as dismissed.

Article 68. Ministers may not assume any salaried office other than that of Minister.

Article 69. The National Consultative Assembly or the Senate shall denounce to the Supreme Court offenses committed by Ministers. The Supreme Court shall conduct a trial in the presence of all its members except when the charge and the suit do not refer to questions relating to Government departments entrusted to them personally, but concern the Minister as a private individual.

Note—So long as the Supreme Court has not been organized, it shall be replaced by a body elected from the members of the two Chambers in equal numbers.

Article 70. When Ministers are impeached by the National Consultative Assembly or the Senate, or accused by private plaintiffs on charges relating to the operation of their departments, the determination of the offenses and penalties to which they are liable shall be regulated by a special law.

✓ ✓ ✓

Powers of the Court

Article 71. The Ministry of Justice and the judicial courts are the Official authority to which public grievances should be submitted; adjudication of religious matters is the function of just and equitable doctors of Islamic theology possessing the necessary qualifications.

Article 72. Disputes concerning political rights come within the jurisdiction of the courts of justice, except as provided by the law.

Article 73. The establishment of temporal tribunals depends on the authority of the law; no one, under any name or on any pretext, may set up a court contrary to the provisions of the law.

Article 74. No court may be held contrary to the provisions of the law.

Article 75. There shall be only one Supreme Court for temporal cases in the capital; it shall no deal with any cases of first instance, except suits versus Ministers.

Article 76. The hearings of all the courts shall be public

except where publicity would be prejudicial to public order or morality. In such a case the court shall declare the necessity of a hearing in camera.

Article 77. In political and press offences, where it is advisable that the proceedings should be private, this must be decided on with the unanimous vote of all the members of the tribunal.

Article 78. The decision handed down by the courts must be substantiated by evidence and proof; and the Article of the law in accordance with which judgment has been rendered must be cited and read in public.

Article 79. In political and press offences, a jury must be present in the courts.

Article 80. The presidents and members of the courts of justice shall be chosen in conformity with the laws of the judiciary and shall be appointed by Royal Decree.

Article 81. No judge of the courts of justice may be provisionally or permanently changed from his office without his case being tried and his offense proved, unless he resigns.

Article 82. A judge of the courts of justice may not be transferred without his own consent. (See interpretation in the footnote.) *

---

* Interpretation of Article 82 of the Supplementary Constitutional Law, voted by the Parliamentary Committee of Judicial Laws on August 18, 1931 (Mordad 26, 1310), and repealed as of November 22, 1952 (Azar, 1331).

Clause 1. Article 82 of the Supplementary Constitutional Law implies that no judge of the courts of justice may be transferred without his own consent from judicial to administrative duties or as an officer attached to the Office of the Public Prosecutor or prosecuting attornies. It would not be a contravention of this Article to change the place of assignment of judges, due regard being given to their grades.

Clause 2. No judge or prosecuting attorney may be assigned more than three years to places where the water and climate are bad, except with his own consent.

No judge or officer attached to the Office of Public Prosecutor or prosecuting attorney having served at posts where the weather is inclement may be assigned to another such post without his own consent for a period of five years from the date of the termination of his assignment at that post.

Each year of service by such officials at posts where the weather is inclement after this law goes into effect shall be calculated as two years at the time of promotion, provided they should have served at least two full years at the said posts.

117

Article 83. The King appoints the Attorney General with the approval of the religious judge.

Article 84. The salaries of members (judges) of the courts of justices shall be fixed by law.

Article 85. The presidents of the courts of justice may not accept salaried State offices, unless they agree to serve without salary and provided such agreement is not inconsistent with the law.

Article 86. A Court of Appeal shall be instituted in the capital of each province for judicial affairs as expressly provided for by the judicial laws.

Article 87. Military courts shall be organized throughout the country in accordance with special laws.

Article 88. Arbitration in cases of dispute as to the limits of the administrations and functions of the State shall be referred to the Supreme Court in accordance with the provisions of law.

Article 89. The Ministry of Justice and the courts shall enforce public orders as well as provincial, district and municipal regulations when they are in conformity with the law.

✓   ✓   ✓

The Provincial and District Councils

Article 90. Throughout the whole Empire provincial and district councils shall be set up in accordance with special regulations. The fundamental laws affecting these councils are as follows:—

Article 91. The members of the provincial and district councils shall be elected directly by the inhabitants in accordance with the regulations of these councils.

Clause 3. Judges whose posts are changed with due regard to Clause 1 of this law, but who refuse to accept their assignment, shall be considered as insubordinate and shall be tried before the disciplinary court and punished in accordance with the regulations of the Ministry of Justice.

Clause 4. The second provision of Article 1 of the law relating to the Employment of Judges and Officers attached to the Office of Public Prosecutor or Prosecuting Attornies voted on March 20, 1928 (Esfand 28, 1306) shall not apply to graduates of the first term of the Judicial Service Class in the Ministry of Justice.

Clause 5. This law shall go into effect as of September 7, 1931 (Shahrivar 15, 1310).

Article 92. The provincial and district councils have the authority to exercise complete supervision over reforms in the public interest, subject to the provisions of the laws in force.

Article 93. The account of the receipts and expenses of all kinds in the provinces and districts shall be printed and published by the councils.

✓ ✓ ✓

FINANCE

Article 94. No tax may be imposed except in accordance with the law.

Article 95. The law shall specify cases of exemption from taxation.

Article 96. The scale of taxation shall be fixed and approved annually by the National Consultative Assembly by a majority of votes.

Article 97. In matters of taxation there shall be no difference or distinction amongst individuals who compose the nation.

Article 98. Exemption from or reduction of taxation shall be the subject of a special law.

Article 99. Apart from cases specifically excepted by the law, no payment may be exacted from the inhabitants on any ground save those decreed as State, provincial, district and municipal taxes.

Article 100. No order may be issued for payment of any allowance or gratuity from the Government Treasury except in accordance with the law.

Article 101. The members of the Accounts Tribunal shall be elected by the National Consultative Assembly for a term to be fixed by law.

Article 102. The Accounts Tribunal is responsible for verifying and controlling the accounts of the Ministry of Finance, and for settling the accounts of all accountants of the Treasury. It shall take particular care to see that no item of the expenditure shown in the budget shall exceed the fixed limits or undergo any change or alteration, and that each sum shall be expended on the object for which it was allocated. At the same time it shall control and audit the various accounts of all departments of the Government and shall collect the vouchers of the accounts. It shall submit to the National Consultative Assembly a statement of all the accounts of the country with its comments appended.

Article 103. The constitution, organization and management of the Tribunal shall be in accordance with law.

✔   ✔   ✔

THE ARMY

Article 104. The law determines the manner of recruiting the army. The duties and rights of the military, as well as their promotions, are regulated by law.

Article 105. Military expenditure shall be approved each year by the National Consultative Assembly.

Article 106. No foreign armed force may be admitted into the service of the State or reside in or pass through any part of its territory except in accordance with the law.

Article 107. The military may not be deprived of their salaries (rights), ranks and dignitaries except in accordance with the law.

COPY OF THE IMPERIAL RESCRIPT

In the Name of God Almighty!

This Supplementary Constitutional Law has been noted and found to be all right. We shall, if God wills, personally guard and watch all its provisions. Our sons and descendants, too, shall support these sacred principles, Insha'Allah!

(Signature of Mohammad Ali Shah Qajar).

Imperial Palace, Tehran,
Sha'ban 29, 1325 lunar year of the Hejira (Mizan 15, 1286 solar year (October 8, 1907).

✔   ✔   ✔

120

RESOLUTION BY THE CONSTITUENT ASSEMBLY

dated May 8, 1949 (Ordibehesht 18, 1328), to Annex an
Additional Article to the Supplementary Constitutional
Law and Modify Article 48 of

THE CONSTITUTIONAL LAW

Whenever the National Consultative Assembly and the Senate separately vote by a two-thirds majority of all their members, either on their own proposal or on a proposition of the Government, the necessity of revising one or several specific articles of the Constitution or of the Supplementary Law, and His Imperial Majesty confirms the opinion of the Chambers, a Constituent Assembly shall be elected and convened by Imperial order.

The Constituent Assembly shall be composed of a number of members equal to the legal total of the National Consultative Assembly and of the Senate. The elections to the Constituent Assembly shall take place according to a law which shall be ratified by the two Chambers. The powers of this Assembly shall be limited to the revision of the article or articles determined by the two Chambers and confirmed by His Imperial Majesty.

The decisions of the Constituent Assembly will require a two-thirds majority of the total number of members and they will be put into execution after approval by His Imperial Majesty.

This article does not affect any of the articles of the Constitution and the Supplementary Law which have reference to the Holy Religion of Islam and the official creed of the country which is the Ja'fari doctrine of the Shi'ah Sect with Twelve Imams and its tenets, or to the Constitutional Monarchy of Iran, which are unchangeable for eternity.

Concerning articles 4, 5, 6, and 7 of the Constitution and the interpretation of Article 7 as well as Article 8 of the Constitution and Article 49 of the Supplementary Constitutional Law and, taking into consideration precedents, and the laws previously enacted in connection with these articles, the National Consultative Assembly and the Senate which will be formed after the ratification of the present article will meet once to revise the said articles immediately after both Chambers officially assume their functions. With this objective, the two Chambers will convene with the President of the Senate in the chair and will decide on the necessary amendments by a majority vote of two-thirds of their total membership. These amendments will be put into effect after they have been confirmed and signed by His Imperial Majesty.

Index

Abadan 79
Achaemenid dynasty 9, 17, 21, 23, 25, 27, 82
Afghans 20, 86
Afshar, Ambassador Amir Aslan 47
Agency for International Development (AID) 56
Ahmad Shah (Qajar) 9, 29, 87
Ala, Hossein 41, 46
Alam, Assadollah 41-43
American Aid to Iran 13, 56, 59, 65, 68
American University 10, 89
Amini, Dr. Ali 41
Amir Kabir 91
Anglo-Iranian Oil Company (AIOC) 65-66
Anglo-Russian Convention (1907) 9, 12, 72, 87
Anglo-Russian-Iranian Treaty (1942) (see Tripartite Treaty) 65, 72, 88
Arabs (Arab World) 18-19, 24-26, 54, 65, 84, 90, 92
art 18, 21, 24-28
Arvand Rud (Shatt-al-Arab) 67, 81
Ataturk, Mustafa Kemal 30-31
Axis 65, 72
Azerbaijan (province, crisis) 12, 33, 43, 65, 72, 80, 88

Baghdad Pact (see CENTO) 12, 67, 72, 88
Bahrain 43, 67, 70
Bakhtiaris 50
balance of payments 57
Baluchis 50

Bank Markazi (Central Bank of Iran) 47, 60
Bank Melli 60
banks 60
bazaar 27, 47, 50-52
Britain 12, 30, 56, 58, 61, 63-67, 69-72, 91-92
Browne, E. G. 26, 28, 46, 92-93
budget 59

capitulations 63, 69
carpets 27, 58
Caspian 64
Celebration of Founding of Iranian Monarchy 74-75
Central Bank of Iran (see Bank Markazi)
Central Treaty Organization (CENTO) 12, 33, 43, 67-69, 72, 88
chai khaneh (tea houses), ghahva khaneh (coffee houses) 52
Constitution 16, 37, 44-45, 87, 94-122
Constitutional Period (Movement) 9, 12, 40, 94
Coronation (1967) 35, 74, 88

Development Corps (Extension and Development Corps) 13, 34, 39, 49, 74
Development Plans (Economic) 34, 53, 55, 57-58, 60-61, 79-80

East Germany 43
Education Corps (Sepha-e Danesh) 13, 34, 39, 49, 55, 73
Eqbal, Dr. Manuchehr 41

123

European Economic Community (EEC) 58
Export-Import Bank 57
Extension and Development Corps (see Development Corps)

Fadayan-i-Islam 33, 35, 40, 46-47
Farah, Empress (Farah Pahlavi) 35
Farah Pahlavi Charity Foundation (1963) 53, 88
Far East 12
France 22, 38, 56, 91

gendarmerie 65, 70
Germany (West) 30, 58, 61, 65, 71
Great Britain (see Britain)
Gross National Product (GNP) 5, 7, 61, 79
Gulistan, Treaty of 63-64, 87

Health Corps 13, 34, 49, 53, 73
Hellenism 18
historiography 16, 89-94
Houses of Justice 74
Hoveyda, Amir Abbas 42, 47
Howard, Harry N. 10

India 20, 22, 71, 86
Iran-e Novin (New Iran Party) 37, 39, 42, 46
Iranian Armed Forces 30, 32-33, 48, 70, 81
Iranian-Soviet Treaty of Friendship (1921) (Russo-Iranian Treaty of Friendship 64-65, 87
Iraq 67
Isfahan 20, 22, 27-28, 52, 93
Islam (Muslim) 10, 12, 18-19, 24, 48-49, 53, 64, 67, 69, 89-90, 92
Ismail Safavi, Shah (see Safavi)
Israel 67-69
Italy 56
International Bank for Reconstruction and Development (IBRD) 57
International Monetary Fund (IMF) 57
Investment 59-60, 79
Investment Law 60
Izmir Summit Conference (1970) 68

Japan 58, 61
Jews 17, 51

Kosygin, Premier 68
Kurds 50, 70

labor 48, 52-53, 55
Land Reform Law (1962) 53
land reforms 13, 33-34, 38-39, 55, 61, 73
Lend-lease Act (1942) 65
Lewis, Bernard 31, 92
libraries 27
Literacy Corps (see Education Corps)
Lurs 50

Majlis 37-38, 41-43, 45, 65-66, 74
Mansur, Hassan Ali 42
Mardom (People's Party) 37-39, 41-42
Melliyun Party 41-42, 46
Meshed 20, 27
Middle East Institute 10
Millspaugh mission 63-64, 69, 87
missionaries 63
Mohammad Reza Shah Pahlavi 10, 13, 15-16, 30, 32-36, 47-49, 68, 71-74, 79, 88, 91
Mongols 19, 85, 93
Monroe Doctrine 63, 69
Mossadegh, Mohammed 33, 35, 40-41, 43, 46, 66
mullahs 34, 44, 48-49, 51-52
museums 27
mysticism (sufism) 28, 90

Nadir Shah 20, 22, 71, 86, 93
National Front 35, 39-43, 46
National Iranian Oil Company (NIOC) 56, 66
NATO 70
New Iran Party (see Iran-e Novin)
Netherlands 56
Nixon, President 68

Oil Consortium 56
Oil industry (petroleum) 13, 33, 43, 46, 56-62, 65-66, 80
Ottoman Empire 19, 20, 71, 92

124

Pahlavi (era, language) 18, 25
Pahlavi dynasty 17, 20-22, 29, 87
Pahlavi Foundation (1958) 53
Pahlavi, Mohammad Reza Shah (see Mohammad Reza Shah)
Pahlavi, Reza Shah (see Reza Shah)
Pakistan 58, 61, 67-68, 70, 92
Pan-Iranist Party 37, 39, 43, 46
Peace Corps 68
Peasants' Congress (1963) 42
"Persian Corridor" 72
Persian Gulf (Khalidj-e Fars) 12, 45-46, 56, 67, 70, 72
Persian Gulf Command 65, 72
Persian language (Farsi) 25
Persian Revolution 40
petroleum (see oil industry)
Plan Organization 47, 55, 58, 61
political parties 44-47
population 54
Profit Sharing Act (1963) 53
Public Law 480   68

Qajar dynasty 10, 12, 21-22, 29, 64, 71, 87
Qashqais 50
Qavam, Ahmad 40, 43

Razmara, Ali 46, 65-66
Red Lion and Sun Society of Iran 53
Regional Cooperation for Development (RCD) 58, 68-70
Reza Pahlavi (Crown Prince) 35
Reza Shah Pahlavi 10, 13, 15, 29-32, 34, 40, 48, 50, 54, 65, 71, 87-88, 91
Russia 10, 20, 30, 63-64, 86-87, 91-92

Safavi, Shah Ismail 19-21, 71, 86, 90, 92
Safavid dynasty 10, 17, 19-23, 27, 86, 90, 93
Saljuqs 26, 27, 85
Sassanid dynasty 10, 17-18, 21, 23, 25, 27, 83
Schwarzkopf mission 65
Sepah-e Danesh (see Education Corps)

Shah Abbas 20, 22, 71, 86, 90, 93
Shatt-al-Arab (see Arvand Rud)
Shiites 19, 28, 38, 50, 89
Shiraz 26-27
Shuster mission 63, 69, 87
social insurance 51, 53, 55
Soviet Union (USSR) 12, 30, 32-33, 40, 58, 64-70, 72, 87
Standard Oil Company of Indiana 56
sufism (see mysticism)
Sunay, President Cevdet (Turkey) 68
Sunnites 19, 22, 50

Tabatabai, Seyyid Zia 40
Tabriz 52
Tehran 27, 32-33, 38, 46, 52
Tehran Conference (1943) 32
Tehran Declaration (1943) 65, 88
tourism 52
trade 58, 61
Trans-Iranian Railway 29
Tripartite Treaty (1942) 65, 72, 88
Tudeh 33, 35, 39-41, 43, 47, 64, 66
Turkey (Turkish) 10, 16, 19, 26, 54, 67-68, 71, 92
Turkmanchai, Treaty of 63, 87

United Nations (UN) 12, 68, 72, 88
UN Security Council 68
United States 11-12, 33, 41, 55-59, 61, 63, 65-70, 72-73
universities 52, 54-55
University of Tehran 14, 35, 54
Upton, Joseph M. 22, 35, 78
USSR (see Soviet Union)

White Revolution 34, 42, 51, 54-55, 73
Wilber, Donald N. 22, 28, 70, 78
Women, role of 13, 39, 51
World War I 10, 13, 29, 64, 71
World War II 13, 32, 64, 72

Yahya, President (Pakistan) 68

Zahedi, Ardeshir 47
Zahedi, Fazollah 33, 41, 46
Zoroastrianism 17-18, 25, 50